Burning Down the Barn

Jay Walden

Books by Jay Walden

Just Add Water
Bad Day at Texas Creek
Burning Down the Barn

Burning Down the Barn

Jay Walden

Jay Walden

Special thanks to Eric Willis for his contribution of the front cover photo.

Front Cover photo, Barn Burning, courtesy of Eric Willis. flickr.12/14/2016.flickr.com/photos/superic/15560813/in/album-374697.

CONTENTS

FOREWORD

If you bought this book thinking that you'd be reading about some dastardly act of arson, then I'm gonna apologize right now. Fact is, none of the stories in here have any direct link to the title. Besides, William Faulkner already covered that story and I'm not about to go and try to top him. The real truth is—I stole the idea for the title from Ray Wylie Hubbard.

Ray released an album in 2009 called A.) Enlightenment B). Endarkenment (Hint: There Is No C.) which he called the worst title ever for an album. To top things off, the cover featured an image of him with a sword in one hand and his decapitated head in the other. Ray described the picture as creepy and weird, even by his standards. I kinda thought the same thing the first time I saw it, until I saw one of his performances where he explained the whole thing.

Seems when he was about 9 years old, his job around

the house was to carry out the trash. As long as you carried out the trash, you stayed under the radar and nobody knew you existed. But, you burn down the barn— one time, and all the relatives that you never knew you had, would drive up and say, "There's the kid that burned down the barn." So the title of the album was horrible and the cover was creepy, but he knew he would get a lot more attention by burning down the barn than taking out the trash.

I went down to Taos, New Mexico a while back to see Ray perform. I really like his music because his songs sound a lot like poetry to me, and some of those lyrics give me inspiration when I'm trying hard at this writing thing. After the show I met him and told him I was writing a book, and that I was going to use *Burning Down the Barn*, for a title. All he said was, "Well, that ought to get their attention." He didn't tell me not to do it. He didn't threaten to sue me, so I guess he's alright with it. I'm going to send him a copy before it goes to final print. If he wants some royalties from it, I'll gladly oblige. I doubt he'll ever be able to do much with the checks he'll be cashing.

La Petit Bonheur

Jay Walden

1 LA PETIT BONHEUR

As the skiff pulled along the dock, his head was still dizzy with turtle grass, coral heads, and fish, and the chop coming in from the northeast slapped at the fiberglass hull with the rhythm of someone beating a drum. Already, he could see her headed their way, tanned legs and blue eyes like little bottomless pools that opened up into the sky. A smile came across his face and it tightened around the corners of his mouth from the sandpaper feel of sunburn and layer of gritty, dry salt. He handed the guide a fold of bills, which he palmed and stuffed into one of the front pockets of his shorts, without bothering to look or count them. Perhaps feeling obligated by the generous tip, the guide broke the silence between them.

"You done good today, boy. You had a good day," he said, as he slapped him on the back.

"I did—we did. You put me on some good fish."

"All in a day's work. Always a pleasure. We'll do it again sometime."

"We will. I'll call you again, the next time I can make it down."

He was tired and his shoulders and back ached, but he was happy, very happy. He had fished well and his satisfaction was obvious and it was something he didn't care to contain.

He unjointed the rod and held the pieces in one hand as she came up on his right, and he wrapped his other arm around her neck pulling her close as she kissed him lightly beneath his ear. As he turned his head to look at her, he felt the coarseness of his stubble and the grainy dry salt on his skin contrast against the softness of her face, and she smiled.

"You need a shave."

"And I could use a shower, too."

"Are you hungry?"

"Starving."

"Let's get something to eat."

"Yes, please."

They walked hand-in hand around the corner and up the sidewalk, her soft laughter mixed with the slight breeze, now coming from behind them. At St. Peter's Episcopal, she sat on the wall beneath a Royal Poinciana and he took a photo while the sun burned at the back of his neck, thinking all the while how lucky he was.

Later that afternoon, they sat up at the bar in the big leather captain's chairs of the Full Moon, down on the corner of Simonton and Catherine, and ate smoked fish and raw oysters with Matouk's sauce, raw horseradish; and fresh key limes, squeezed out into the shell. The beer was icy cold, the coldest in town.

As the sun was setting, they lay in the sand at Dog Beach on the Atlantic side, looking up at the clouds that were being pushed farther and farther toward the horizon and he pointed out the odd images of cats, dogs, famous people, trains, and cars— shapes, she could never see.

"I could lie here forever," she said.

"Me too, but we need to go soon," he whispered, as he turned his head and saw that her eyes were closed, noticing how her sun-bleached hair blended with the sugary sand as if it went on forever, as if something beautiful could arise out of it and consume the both of them.

That night the room was hot and she had fallen asleep in the crook of his arm. The white linen curtains moved like old ghosts inside the open window and you could hear the dry rustle of the wind in the palmettos, below. Her hair was damp around her face and at the base of her neck, and a single drop of sweat had formed just below her nose, where her lip was upturned. He stared up through the heat, and sweat, and humid air as the ceiling fan tossed around light and shadows about the room, and wondered just how long forever was.

When he awakened, the room was hot and bright with the sunshine coming through the thin, worn curtains. He was not there. He was not anywhere. He was just an old man that had fallen asleep in the recliner, in the afternoon. The ceiling fan whirred above and the dog was snoring in the corner. Outside, someone was mowing the lawn.

An Appalachian Tale

Jay Walden

2 AN APPALACHIAN TALE

Danny was the fireboss on the hoot-owl shift at Clinchfield Coal's Moss Number 3 mine, down off Gravel Lick Road; worked his way up from a brattice man on first shift; started right out of high school. He worked all night and farmed all day; and by the time he had life all figured out, it was over— his very existence and soul snuffed out and asphyxiated like oxygen from a section full of blackdamp. He left behind a lifetime of slagheaps, a widow, Doreen, and a son, Danny Jr., that everyone just called June.

June never did amount to much; even less so, once Danny was gone. The farm, which had been a good source of income, went all but ignored on account of June being too feeble-minded, a trait everyone on Danny's side of the family attributed to his momma's people, the Taylors. Most folks that knew him, knew the real truth—that he was just plumb sorry and no good, had never struck a lick at a snake in his life, much less at work. After Danny died, he wouldn't even renew the tags on the pickup, just spray- painted Farm Use on the back bumper and drove it anywhere he wanted to go anyway, ignoring the legality of it all. His only contribution to the family income was what little money he brought in from sanging, which was the only time you'd catch him with a hoe in his hand, despite the enormous garden Doreen always planted. Once a month, like clockwork, during the spring, summer, and early fall, June would take down his ginseng, goldenseal, bloodroot, mayapple, lobelia, and crushed aluminum cans to the scrap yard in Norton where they bought recycled metal and herbs; outside of that, he never turned a hand to honest work. The rest of the time he just relied on Danny's miners' pension and his momma's Social Security check when he needed money. I guess it was one of those times that he was coming back from the scrap yard that I first hear him tell that story of his.

We were all sitting on the front porch of Lucille's little jot 'em down store, which was no more than her tiny house with the front room converted to shelves of canned goods, honey buns, candy bars, a few packs of nabs, and a loaf of bread or two. There was an old pop cooler that had a sliding metal lid on the top, that sat right under the front window with a bottle opener on the side, and an old Philco V-Handle refrigerator against the back wall where she kept lunch meat (which amounted to mostly a roll of baloney, and some pre-packaged slices of American cheese); and that, was about it.

My uncle John Brown had built the place and Lucille had taken it over when he moved out after his drunken brother-in-law shot him by jamming a shotgun barrel through the crack in the front door, trying to force his way in. John, or Durb, as we called him, staggered out to the front porch, then stumbled and fell into the ditch, where his brother-in- law, Utchie, stood over him with the gun, making sure he'd killed him. My mom told me he would have died, if he hadn't learned in the Navy how to stop the bleeding by putting pressure on his brachial artery that was spurting blood in the gravel so forceful that he could hear it. Utchie must have thought that Durb was a goner, because he finally walked away, not knowing that he'd only blown off a bigger part of his bicep. I remember seeing that big ugly scar one summer when he wore a t-shirt while he was re-shingling our house.

I think the whole damn town was happy when Utch moved up in Possum Holler with that Cherokee woman that barely spoke any English. Occasionally, you'd hear he'd knifed somebody down at one of the beer joints in St. Paul, but we were glad he didn't come to our town anymore, just sent the Indian woman who walked the entire five- mile round- trip and could only say, "Him's needs cigarettes." He was as mean as a striped snake and we were glad to have him gone. Anyway, we were all sitting out on the porch when June drove up and went inside for the Nehi orange that he always drank.

Greaser— Earl Chafin, was always needling everybody; always trying to get a rise out of someone or another. He was good at it, had nicknamed everyone in town, including himself. He had plenty of faults of his own; never tied his boots, just walked on the strings; and he cut the necks out of his t-shirts when they got too dirty, which drove his wife, Nita, half-crazy. Her favorite line to my mother was always, "Dag-gone 'ol Earl, too lazy to tie his own shoes." Outside of fox hunting and drinking liquor all night, and always poking fun at everyone else, Grease, didn't do much else, but that never stopped him from always messin' with folks and June was no exception.

I'm not a hundred per-cent sure how it all came about, but I know that Grease said something to June about borrowing some of that money he'd just gotten from selling his herbs and all those crushed cans, and that did it. June got hot under the collar right away, I remember that because his face turned beet-red and he took to stuttering, like he always did when he was riled. Grease never let up, because he knew he was getting June's goat, and that's what he lived for— annoying someone until he got'em pissed, but he always did it in good fun; you just had to know how to take him. We all knew he was kidding, but June didn't take it that way, especially when Grease told him he was gonna start following him to find out where he was digging all that ginseng. That put him over the edge and that's when June started in on his story.

June allowed as to how nobody would want to go back where he'd been sanging, because he'd seen the Devil, himself, back in there, said he'd heard some noise coming from a big crack in the ground and when he looked down in there he saw the Devil hoppin' across from lid to lid on all sorts of old coffee cans that he kept down there filled with religion. Apparently, there was equal representation of all religions as well as coffee brands, because he went into detail, recalling all the different kinds—Folger's, Maxwell House, Nescafe', Eight O'Clock, Yuban, JFG, you name it, even an old Hill's Brothers can, too. None of us thought to ask him how he knew there was religion in all those cans, maybe because we were all laughing too hard when Grease said you could always tell when he was lying because his lips were moving, which sent June to the truck that he fired up and spun out in the gravel parking lot and out onto the blacktop, leaving us all staring at Farm Use spray-painted on the back bumper. June became scarce as hen's teeth after that, just stayed around home most of the time, when he wasn't in the woods digging sang.

It must have been a few months after all of that happened, around early or mid-October, because I'd gone bird hunting that day. I'm pretty sure it was October, and I remember I had to go through a bunch of dry milk thistles at the edge of the railroad track and the seeds with all their little white tufts were all over my jacket; that, and there were pawpaws on the ground in the patch just past the fence line that were soft as ripe mushmellons. I remember, too, that the game trail up the Childress Hill that I always used, was still damp on account that side never saw much sun that time of year.

That trail was steep from the get go, full of leaves— red, yellow, brown, and gold, all blending into one giant patchwork— damp and quiet, good so you wouldn't wild flush a bird. Once you got on top, you just walked out the ridge; easy walking, in a mix of poplar, beech, and hickory, with a fair amount of thickets full of possum grapes that the birds liked after they sweetened up, the way they always did once they'd been frosted on a time or two. I walked the fence line next to Bobby Joe's empty tobacco patch once I got on top because it was easier going and you could make better time, and cover more country that way. I remember seeing his tobacco hanging in the barn and the cut-off stumps of his plants in the field that were already brown, so that's another reason I was thinking it was around October. I stayed to the fence line for the first part of the way out the hill, and if I saw a thicket that looked like I could get through it without too much trouble, I waded in, hoping to flush up a bird or two; otherwise, I skirted the thick stuff that was full of old dead and dying kudzu vines and sawbriars that would eat you alive.

I don't think the sun ever did come out that day and the wind had a little bite to it, one of those days that looks like it's gonna turn off fair after the morning, but just gets colder as the day goes on. Still it was good weather to bird hunt in and you'd stay plenty warm as long as you kept walking, which is what bird hunting is, when you do it without dogs.

Down where you could see some muscadine, and fox grape vines had taken over a stand of small hickories, I heard my first grouse drumming and I walked him up, until he flushed nearly at my feet. Shotgun to shoulder— instinct, I swung the old double barreled Ithaca down on him, although he'd gotten twenty yards on me on the flush, and saw a flutter of feathers drift down like oversize snowflakes, as the bird went end over end. I smiled as I lowered the twelve gauge, the one Uncle B.J. had handed down to me, with its double hammers; the weathered stock now down to raw wood where the comb had come to cheek so many times, the checkering on the splinter forend nearly gone from years of use, the blueing just beyond, worn and non-existent up where the hand could be closer to the bore and to line of sight, better for hand-to-eye coordination, unlike an old beavertail design.

My ears were still ringing when I found my bird and he was still warm, so I just put a foot on each wing and pulled on the legs, and the breast pulled right out, clean and slick as a whistle. I was glad he'd landed out in the open, and breast-up; to boot, which made him a lot easier to find. I'd have needed a D-9 dozer to get back in that thicket. I kept walking the hill out and jumped two more birds before the hill dropped off into Possum Holler, one that I never saw; but heard, the other that was just too far out for a shot.

It was getting on into late afternoon and I figured I still had plenty enough time to make a round out towards Bald Knob and back, and still get back home before dark; but I could see Utch's little tarpaper house down below me next to the creek, and I wasn't about to go down that way, although it looked like nobody was at home. My luck, he'd be laid up in there drunk as Cooter Brown and it wasn't worth the shortcut just to save a little time and maybe get myself killed, or have to shoot that sorry son-of-a-bitch. Instead, I decided I'd just walk back out the ridge until it cut the old logging road that Bobby Joe used to get his tractor up to his farm. I'd cross the creek at the bottom, down where he'd put a bunch of rocks on the upper side to spread the water and shallow out the creek, to make a ford— live to hunt another day.

About an hour later, on the way out to the knob, I had another bird bust on me early in some thick cover that I never got a bead on, but I kicked up a double with one of them banking out in the open of an old clear-cut, giving me a perfect swing-through shot. That one locked his wings and sailed a ways from the point where I'd hit him. By the time I found him, I could see wood smoke rising from a few ridges over, people were coming home, cooking dinner—there's nothing that warms like a fireplace or old wood stove after a long cold day in the woods; lights would be coming on soon—comfort. I broke down the gun and laid the butt over my shoulder, and started back the way I'd come.

I knew right away that I'd stayed later than I intended and that I'd have to walk the last part of the way home in the dark. I wasn't too worried; though, that part would be out in the open and level, along the railroad tracks. If I double-timed it back out the logging road I could make it to the two track that ran down Possum Holler and be at the railroad crossing before pitch dark. I picked up my pace and stretched out my stride— thinking about those birds in a cast iron skillet, about a fire in the wood stove.

Looking back now, the smart thing would have been to stay on the logging road until it met up with the two track that ran down the holler, but I was anxious to get back home—too anxious. It was getting darker by the moment back in there, and I could see the two track, faintly below; down the steep hillside, so I stepped off the logging road and headed straight toward the bottom. What I didn't count on was that it would be so much darker in the woods, and as I stumbled over rocks that I couldn't see, and slid in the thick leaves, I ended up smack-dab in the middle of a sawbriar patch that grabbed at my pant legs and coat like a wildcat, the more I fought it. By the time I thrashed my way out, I was sweatin' like a whore at a weenie roast, and plumb out of breath. I bent over to get my wind back, still holding on to the shotgun barrel in that last moment of twilight; just before darkness takes its dominion over light— that special moment when it feels like the finger of God touches and ignites your very soul, and saw the two track just below me, as the hill dropped off into a steep embankment.

My legs were wobbly from walking all day and stumbling all over the hill, and fighting that briar patch, but the sight of that little road gave me new spirit and I tore a beeline down towards it without a second thought. Just as I got to the bottom, my momentum got away from me and my legs were going all catawampus, when the toe of my boot caught an old grapevine, and before you could say Jack Robinson, I went ass over teakettle out into the road. The shotgun flew off my shoulder and went rattling out into the rocks, and I never even had a chance to get my hands out in front of me to break my fall. My head landed on the rocks in one of the tracks, and the impact had completely knocked the wind out of me, so I just laid there in the road trying to get my wits back. When I stood up I was facing up the road and my head was bleeding like a stuck hog. I could see the old Vienna sausage can that everyone used as a dipper, there on an upturned stick at the Prestly spring, shiny, the way the glint of something unnatural always stands out in the woods; catches your eye in a heartbeat, just like movement will do. I was dizzy, my pants were torn at the knees, my legs ached, I had blood running into one eye, but there was no mistaking what I saw next.

Up in the tall grass to the side of the road, I saw the figure of a man, or something like a man, on his hands and knees, kneeling there with his head down to the water, drinking from the spring. Perhaps he sensed me or didn't care if I was there, but when he rose up on his knees and turned his torso to face me, I could see that he was unclothed and as pale as if he had fallen into a flour barrel. The thing I remember most, were his eyes— coal black without any whites like a normal man, riveting and cold that seemed to burn straight through me, so that it made the hair on the back of my neck stand up. That look— that look that I shall never forget— turned my blood to ice water and I stood as a stone, unable to move, unable to breathe, knowing the true feeling of terror. How long we were locked in that gaze I don't know to this day, but the only thing that broke it, was him springing from that position with the leap of a deer, onto the bank beyond. In two more bounds, in a distance I could not judge because it appeared so great, he was gone into the darkness that had fallen onto the woods.

I stood there, still staring, staring at the surrounding jet obsidian that seemed to suck the very essence of illumination from the world; again, I do not know how long. My hands were trembling and I felt as if I would faint, somehow knowing, feeling, that I had just seen the very incarnate of evil. Finally, I turned, and finding the shotgun, jammed both barrels with shells and heard laughter from the darkness behind me, like the sound of the hoot of an owl. I broke into a run and never slowed until I reached home.

Winter came and went, and still I told nothing of my story, although I thought or dreamed of it nearly every night. That eerie vision came and went like the dark clouds that came scudding over the ridges of darkened Appalachian timber, barren of leaves and color; my soul at times as cold as the snow they bore. My sleep was fitful and I was more anxious for spring, and the light I knew it would bring, than I could ever remember.

I steered clear of town for as long as possible and I wondered if somehow it had been an unconscious move on my part, to keep from unburdening myself with that story I'd been living with, haunting me since back in the fall. I had no real intention of ever telling anyone, but sometimes when you keep things all bottled up for too long, they end up spilling out anyway, even when you don't want 'em to.

As time passed ever so slowly, early April eventually arrived and I finally had to make that trip to the county co-op to get a load of salt for the water softener— that trip I had dreaded for so long. Once I'd placed my order, Ron Barrett said he'd load it in the pickup while I stayed inside and paid. As I was standing at the counter, I saw June down at the far end with his back turned to me looking at bailing twine, probably to tie up his lobelia; when he turned, our eyes met and I could tell right away, he knew. We never spoke a word; but he knew, he knew what I'd seen that October day up in the woods, knew just the same as if I'd told him word for word myself. And I knew it too, knew that he understood; there was no mistaking the mutual comprehension, the familiarity we shared, knowing what would return to us like chilled winds that claim the darkness on the other side of men's unwanted dreams, dreams that could not be wished away. The cashier handed me my change and I stuck it in my pocket, and walked outside toward the truck. I waved to the guys on the loading dock, forcing a smile I really didn't believe in, already dreading the thought of trying to get to sleep at night.

Nothing Left to Lose

3 NOTHING LEFT TO LOSE

November came rolling out of the South San Juans, all dark clouds, heavy with the regret of autumn and full of thunder, scattering the last dry leaves of the big cottonwoods like inconsequential, poor papier-mache imitations. It was a lonesome time, as lonely as last call, and I stood in the willows with my back braced to it, everything about me feeling old, except for the eyes— green, reflecting back green of the stream, and promise. This was to be a big El Niño year and the tops of the mesas were already dusted with snow, the dark pinions standing out like you'd see on some dime store Christmas card. It should have been a comforting scene, but all I could get out of it was that certain sadness that comes with an early winter, the kind that leaves you feeling you don't quite have both hands on the wheel, when the sun didn't shine, and the phone wouldn't ring.

Everywhere else it was all turkey and stuffing, and pumpkin spice everything, and resentment arose in me against it all, that Norman Rockwell image of the family around the table, a fire burning in the hearth, although I knew I'd done it to myself. I reached around to my waistpack and felt a cold lump of ham and cheese sandwich, and hoped I'd be alright with all of it somehow.

As I stepped out onto the edge ice, it tinkled like fine porcelain breaking, and the ripples slapped underneath the cut-bank with the sound of a dog lapping a water bowl. The wind came through the cottonwoods again, and I looked upstream to see Aaron coming around the island, gloved hands on the oars of the big Clack that he rows, scooting river right to give me a wider berth than I really needed, had I already been fishing. There were two sports fore and aft, bundled and humped up on the seats like sitting hens, both hands in their jacket pockets. He grinned when he saw it was me, put a few stokes in with his heavy shoulders as he glided within earshot.

"You doin' any good?"

"Just got here," I said.

"There's some risers, up in the flats."

I nodded my thanks; I'm sure that's all he expected, and he dipped back deep on the oars again as he exhaled, his breath a fog in the cold air. I could see frost on his beard.

The sports never spoke, just stayed humped up as they went around the next corner toward Death Row, maybe disappointed they didn't have the skills to tackle those rising fish they'd passed up. Maybe they were on a half-day and just wanted to get back to the lodge where it was warm, sorry they'd picked the coldest day in November and a 7:00 a.m. start time. Whatever it was, I knew it wasn't Aaron's fault; he had too many repeat clients that were always into fish, to have any complainers. Anyway, you couldn't help but like the guy, ran a couple of liver head pointers on birds up in Montana, when he could get away from the guide business, which wasn't often enough. Understood the world, the way I understood the world, the importance of good bird dogs and knowing where all the best fish were, had his priorities in order, kept things simple.

I spent the rest of the day up in the flats, casting to fish that rose about everywhere to a mix of midges and BWOs. The wind came and went with intervals, sometimes when it didn't seem to make sense to do it anymore; when the fish were put down by the chop, and I thought a couple of times about leaving for home to try and write, but I felt it was still too early. I was afraid of my mood and knew I probably wouldn't make it for the same reason I'd never been a lawyer— I couldn't pass the bar. I'd stay late until I was sure it was closed and eliminate the possibility.

I got home and the house was dark and her rental car was gone, but I didn't read too much into it, just figured she'd gotten bored and went into town, maybe for more wine and groceries. I left the rod and my net in the truck for tomorrow and grabbed my pack because my cell phone was in there. Across the fence, I heard the dog's nails clicking on the concrete, heard his whine like always when the truck door shut. I reached across the fence to undo the latch and he licked my hand like usual, all part of his routine. As I plopped down on the ratty old couch I kept out there, he laid his head in my lap for a pet, sniffed my waders, and then headed around the corner to the back yard, to do whatever he always does back there to keep himself amused.

I scooted up to the edge of the couch to undo my laces that were frozen and remembered the conversation we'd had about the thing; the fact that she wanted it hauled off to the dump, my protest that it was part of my Appalachian heritage, that all true hillbillies needed to have living room furniture on the porch— the dump trip wasn't happening. The ice on the laces stung my already freezing hands and I couldn't wait to get the damn things off, get out of those cold, wet waders and into the house where it was warm.

I hung my lanyard and sunglasses on the pegs over the light switch in the kitchen and flipped the switch as the dog followed me in, threw the other switch down the hallway, with him at my heels. Back in the bedroom, I peeled off my fleece pants and went looking for my Carhartts, that's when I noticed that the closet door had been left open and all her clothes were gone. Initially I wasn't all that surprised, this wasn't my first rodeo. I knew I was a hard man to live with, but it stung enough to nearly make me nauseous when I let myself dwell on it too much. I slipped on the jeans and shut the closet door as I left the room and headed for the kitchen. If I was going to be lonely, I wasn't about to do it on an empty stomach.

I pulled a Tupperware container full of elk chili out of the fridge and put it in a saucepot I grabbed from the cabinet, then dropped in one of those big ice cubes I keep in the freezer for a heavy tumbler that's just about perfect for three fingers of bourbon. I dug deep down into the vegetable drawer and came out with a couple fresh jalapenos, which I drenched in olive oil and covered in coarse salt, and went back out to the patio and fired up the grill, taking my drink along, because I really needed it just now. I laid the peppers out on the grates to roast and went back inside to stir up the cornbread mixture they were going in. Things weren't out of hand just yet, but I was well into my second bourbon; neat, because the ice had melted, when the phone rang.

I looked at the caller i.d., and then answered like I didn't know who'd be calling. Her voice was low and soft; but not in an apologetic kind of way, just full of sincerity, something I'd always been told I lacked.

"How are you?" I asked.

"I'm fine." "Fine."

The repetition and the second emphasis, told me it wasn't so.

We made small talk about the weather and the fishing for a while, but I could feel there was a shit storm building and I was about to get caught in the epicenter.

When she let it go— it just flowed like water, crystal clear and cold, like some brookie stream way up in the high country.

"You know that day on the river we spent together? I would have married you on the spot, if you'd asked. I wouldn't have cared if it had been by a medicine man or a shaman; I would have done it in a minute. You screwed up by not asking me to stay. You could have had it all."

I knew exactly what she was talking about. There was silence mixed with sad realization on my end and I was just about to say something, but my lips wouldn't work, and then I noticed the phone was dead because she'd hung up.

That night when I crawled into bed, the sheets were cold and I could hear the wind rattling the fence outside; the front was passing through and the weather was changing.

The next morning I was standing at the kitchen window with the hard light of winter's dawn coming up strong in the east. There was an inch and a half of slush on the pickup when I put the key in the door. I backed out of the driveway and turned left toward the river. The sky rolled out before me like blue, wholesale carpet and you could see clear up to Colorado, where the snow was deep on the peaks.

I'd handled my life so far with all the grace and charm

of a hemorrhoid operation. I didn't have a damn clue how I was going to handle this.

B.C.

Jay Walden

4 B.C.

It was only the second week of September, but I knew it was time to leave Alaska. I'd been watching winter chasing fall from the mountainside; from across the river, the snowline creeping closer and closer to town each day. The silvers were in and the fishing was good; I knew I'd have to force myself to go, or be stuck here for the winter. My fishing partner for the last five months had already left a week ago, flown back to Colorado; I'd be driving back by myself, if you didn't count the company of the dog.

Five months of solid fishing and I still couldn't get enough of it. I hoped to catch the winter steelhead moving in, down in British Columbia, but right now I really had to get the hell out of Dodge. The thought of spending a winter up here, was something my mind wouldn't even entertain.

Part of me would miss this valley, its rivers, its fish, and most of its people (as odd and quirky as they were); most who would stay behind because they wanted to, or needed to. There were others who had no choice—could never go back home again— for reasons that were mostly of the legal variety. Regardless of guilt or innocence, their sentence was all the same— four months of darkness and sub-zero temperatures. It was not a club of which I wished to become a member.

On my way out of town the next morning, a cold wind blew brown leaves across the highway and there were already a couple of inches of slushy snow on the ground. The mix of rain and wet snow on the windshield made me wonder if perhaps I'd pushed the envelope just a little too far this time. Further north, about an hour out of Anchorage, the weather finally broke and it was fall again; I whispered a little prayer under my breath that it would hold for a while.

I spent my last night in the Last Frontier in the same small town I'd spent my first, sleeping out in the open, staring up at the stars in a campground in Tok. I didn't know it at the time, but those accommodations would prove to be on the luxury scale for the next three days until I reached Smithers, B.C.

I'd read a little about this drive I was about to take across the Yukon Territory, then down the Cassiar Highway (B.C. Highway 37) through British Columbia. I knew the last leg; the Cassiar Highway, was the northwesternmost highway in B.C. bisecting some of the most remote areas of the province. I knew it was mostly asphalt with a few gravel sections and no passing lanes, and one lane bridges. I knew it was scenic and led down to Smithers where the steelhead might be. I had a sleeping bag and a pad, a tent, water, coffee, two, full, five- gallon gas cans, Ramen noodles and summer sausage, a bottle of hot sauce, a fly rod, and a hundred and thirty pound Shiloh Shepherd. What I didn't have was a gun. I had to ship that home from Alaska— Canada is picky about that sort of thing. All I cared about was the scenic and steelhead part.

Traveling through the Yukon, I did a lot of thinking, looking at that barren, hostile land— wondering why or how anyone could live up here, and what had possessed people to come in the first place, gold or no gold. During the Pleistocene Age it was home to North America's megafauna— dire wolves, steppe bison, mastodons, and smilodon (a saber toothed cat weighing up to 600 pounds.) Humans had inhabited the area since the Ice Age, some 20,000 years ago. I stared at the blue glaciers and peak, after seemingly endless peak, of the Wrangell-St Elias range and marveled how little had changed. You could fit Switzerland, Yellowstone, and Yosemite, within the borders of the National Park there. From the looks of the place, I wouldn't be surprised if there were a smilodon or two still roaming around somewhere in those mountains.

Eleven hours out of Tok, I was bleary- eyed and nodding off at the wheel, but I had reached the Yukon/B.C. border. At the intersection of YT1/Alaska Highway and the Cassiar, I stopped at the Beaver Post gas station and convenience store to fill up and double check the gas cans. From this point on, these little places would be few and far between and if you arrived too late in the evening, low on fuel, you were stuck there until they opened the following morning. I topped off the tank and walked inside to pay.

The guy behind the counter was overly chatty like the Prime Minister of Canada had just walked in on him, unannounced. I did my best to humor him with conversation, although I was champing at the bit to get on the road again and find a camp spot before nightfall. As he was going on and on about one thing or another and I was looking for a pause in his non-stop yammer to make my getaway, my eyes drifted outside to the view of a vast landscape void of any evidence of human life. The view fully explained the chatter and I understood why he was milking every occasion possible to it fullest for personal interaction, before winter set in. I wondered what you said to the same person that you'd been shut inside with, after the third month of 20 hours of darkness, sub-zero temperatures, and a view out the window of nothing but snow. I hadn't a clue; I was just glad that it wouldn't be me. When I finally broke away, he followed me to the door and was still talking in the doorway as I pulled back onto the highway. I looked down the narrow road that ran for the next 450 miles through some of the most rugged and uninhabited country in North America, took a deep breath, and turned on to it.

By now it was getting late and I was exhausted from the drive. I needed to sleep, just pitch the tent in the first clearing I came to or lay the sleeping pad and bag out under the stars; I didn't plan on being too particular. There was certainly no shortage of woods;

I just needed a place to get the Jeep off the highway. That's when I saw my first bear and that changed everything.

Particular or not, I wasn't about to set up here for the night. I needed some distance between me and that big black man-eater before I could ever close my eyes, so I drove on, despite my fatigue. Twenty miles later, a grizzly and two cubs crossed the road fifteen yards in front of me and I realized I was gonna need a new plan. I made it another fifteen miles, but it didn't matter anymore; I wasn't going to sleep outside tonight. I got it; I wasn't at the top of the food chain; there were bears out there, apparently a lot of them. I'd spent the last five months in a tent in Alaska, with a gun at my fingertips; there was no way I was going to do it here unarmed. I pulled off at the next wide spot in the road with a new plan in mind.

They say that if plan B were ever worth a damn, it would be plan A; but the way I saw it, my options were severely limited. There were no motels, no campgrounds, no gas station parking lots, no houses or driveways, and the last car I had passed had gone by over an hour ago. I was tired, but not tired enough to try and sleep outside; I was spooked.

Eventually, I had it all worked out and plan B went something like this: my only alternative was to try and stretch out across the console and bucket seats in the Jeep and try to get what shut-eye I could manage. The dog in the back with all my camping and fishing equipment would function as my bear alarm in the event of a nighttime sneak attack; I'd leave the keys in the ignition for a speedy get away at the first sign of a bark.

I'd slept in some uncomfortable places before but this one took the prize. The center console was poking me in the ribs, and I didn't dare get into the sleeping bag in fear that it would impede my hasty escape, should I need to make one. I put on my down jacket and wool cap and bunched up part of the sleeping bag over the console to give my ribs a little relief and discovered that if I put the stick shift into third gear it gave me a little more leg room. I rehearsed the escape plan over and over in my mind, complete with the vivid image of giant bear claws slicing through the plastic windows of the Jeep as I sped away in a cloud of dust and gravel. I especially drilled home the part about remembering to switch back into first gear before trying to pull away. I knew it would have been safer to have left the Jeep in first gear, but I figured I'd already made enough concessions where comfort was concerned and I really wanted that extra leg room. I was quite certain I could remember one small detail if my life depended on it.

When I awoke the next morning it was just around daylight. I felt like I had been in a gang fight and my gang hadn't shown up. The keys dangling in the ignition were like a wake-up call, reminding me of where I was and why I'd subjected myself to such cruel and unusual punishment for a few hours of sleep. I looked around for a moment, relieved that none of the windows were slashed from bear claws. The dog sat up and stretched, and looked at me like the crazy person that I probably was. I fished out my thermos that was still half-full of yesterday's coffee. It was tepid and tasted like the nectar of the gods. I checked the surrounding area outside for any man-eating creatures that might do me harm, and satisfied that the coast was clear, put the dog on his leash and went for a bathroom break. After a short walk and a lot of stretching that didn't involve going into the woods, we both piled back into the vehicle and headed south again.

To call the view along this highway scenic was the understatement of all understatements. Everything up here was huge— the trees were huge; the mountains were huge; the rivers, even at their low fall levels, were massive giant floodplains of boulders with islands of rock the size of football fields, scattered throughout, with piles of logjams the size of houses. There were miles and miles of untouched, pristine wilderness and endless snowcapped peaks, with lakes, rivers, and streams stretched across the landscape everywhere. I'd seen some of the best the Rockies had to offer in the American west, but this was on a whole different scale. These were not mere mountains, but monolithic massifs, the earth's crust forced up to meet the sky, pockmarked with avalanche chutes and baleful grey granite—awe inspiring. I pulled to the side of the highway and stepped outside, trying to take it all in. I stood there, frozen in time, with the rush of wind in the sway of hundred-year-old trees, followed by the silence of nothingness.

Country that big and that raw can have an effect on you— look at it too long and it will carry you into it, make you feel insignificant, and you'll lose your place in the worldly order of things. I couldn't keep my eyes off of those distant vistas where there were no roads, where probably no human had ever trod. I wondered what it would feel like to be up there, alone. I wondered what it looked like from the top, what was on the other side? I left and drove on for hours, passing only an occasional logging truck. It was late in the season and all the tourists that might possibly travel this road were gone. I had the wilderness to myself. It was superb.

At Dease Lake (population 400 and the largest community in northwest B.C.) I stopped for gas, filled up the thermos again, and grabbed enough convenience store food to constitute what I was going to consider lunch. The place looked deserted. Perhaps the sign along the highway that stated— Winter tire and chain regulations in effect from October 1 till March 31— had something to do with it. Maybe everyone had left town to get their chains and snow tires. Maybe they were out gathering wood to prepare for the entire thirty-eight hours of sunshine they were going to receive during the whole month of December. I didn't worry about it much; I had somewhere else I needed to be. I was back out on the highway and in the wilderness again in no time flat.

By late afternoon, I was drowsy from my lack of sleep the night before. The coffee and the scenery helped a little, but I had a lot to overcome after being balled up on those two little bucket seats all night, tossing and turning, trying to get comfortable enough to doze off, keeping one eye open for a possible bear attack. The sun made its arc through the sky and another day had passed. By evening; as I was looking for another place to park and spend the night, the bears were out again— everywhere, in groups of four, sometimes five or six, eating berries on the banks of the highway, oblivious to my passing car. Hyperphagia it's called— eating with reckless abandon, like there may not be another berry or salmon tomorrow, packing on up to four pounds of weight gain per day, consuming up to 20,000 calories a day if you're a big grizzly; and some of them were. They'd be drinking water like nobody's business, urinating up to four gallons in 24 hours; getting ready for winter and the big sleep, while denying me mine. I was jealous, I felt like I could lie down and sleep till spring, my eyelids were heavy, and my ribs hurt. I wondered what Smithers would be like; I wondered if the steelhead were in.

I so wanted to get to Smithers that night. I wanted to sleep in a real bed for the first time in five months. I wanted a hot shower. I wanted a real meal, and I wanted to be away from these bears. Instead, I found myself drifting off the road from time to time, nodding off. I was scaring myself, afraid I might fall asleep at the wheel; it was getting dark, Smithers and the steelhead I hoped to find there, were still about three hours away. I knew right then and there that I wouldn't make it— not tonight.

I settled instead for a roadside rest stop, a paved one this time, with restrooms, but no flush toilets, though. I was getting closer to civilization, but I wasn't quite there yet. Somehow the sight of a paved parking lot and a building with a toilet gave me an increased sense of security; even if it was a false one. That such an obscure thing as a crapper can give you hope when you're desperate, defies logic, I know; but over the years I have found that my mind works in strange ways, when I'm alone. Anyway, I just couldn't see any self-respecting bear attacking me here in a paved parking lot. I ate some summer sausage and crackers, fed the dog, and then put the Jeep into third gear and curled up across the seats again.

When I awoke the next morning, it was foggy and the parking lot was wet. It had rained during the night, but I hadn't heard it. I polished off the rest of the coffee from the thermos, took the dog and myself for a bathroom break, and then headed out— glad that I had survived another night and thankful for the faint signs of civilization that had helped to make that possible. A hundred yards down the road, a big, lanky black bear crossed the road in the fog in front of me, taking his time like he owned the place; which in a way, he did. This whole bear thing was beginning to look like some kind of bad joke.

At the small village of Kitwanga (the people of the place of the rabbits, in the native tongue) my 450 mile odyssey down the Cassiar Highway had finally reached its end. From this point on, the Cassiar (B.C.Highway 37) becomes B.C. Highway 16 continuing east to Prince George, or west into the Bulkley Valley toward Smithers. The drive down the broad valley going west opens up to some beautiful country, lush and green, interspersed with ranch land, backed by snowcapped mountains— a sight that'll take your breath away. The drive so far had been a memorable, visual experience and the views from the valley with its green fields bordered by aspens and maples all aglow in the full radiance of fall color; and the rugged mountains beyond, just topped everything off. The occasional ranch house in the distance bore a conventional mark that I was reentering civilization again, something that I was glad to see, glad for all the comforts it could offer, one of which was radio reception and music.

Now that I was approaching the real world, I switched on the radio that had been useless for the last two days and was surprised that I could dial in a station that came in static free— CFBV—Moose FM, adult contemporary straight out of Smithers, not my particular favorite genre, but at least it was sound. After two songs, the news came on—local news with a lead story of a husband and a wife that had been found the day before, killed by a grizzly. It was too much, I couldn't take it anymore. I switched off the radio and stared out the windows at all that wilderness again as if somehow I might see that moose camp I'd just heard about, somewhere up below the snowline, a needle in an endless haystack of Engelmann and Sitka spruce with two lonely hunters torn limb by limb, by some savage beast. Were they terrified out of their wits when it happened? Had they fought back? Where were their guns? Did a bear rip through their tent in the middle of the night? A million thoughts and questions raced through my mind. I felt that view of the remote mountains pull at me again, and that harsh, wild countryside with its forlorn solitude of vastness swept me in, and swallowed me up.

When I reached Smithers the first thing I did was get a motel room and call my friend Joe back in Colorado at Duranglers Fly Shop. If anyone would have the skinny on the steelhead around this place, Joe was the guy— he'd fished and guided up here for years. I lucked out, he was there and he answered the phone. He gave me the name and the location of a fly shop in town and offered a couple of local guide's names. I wrote down the names, knowing that my budget wouldn't tolerate a guide fee and a tip, no matter how much I probably needed one. I'd only fished for steelhead once before, on the Anchor River in Alaska, but the fish weren't in yet, so that really didn't count. I'd read and heard enough about it that I was sure I could figure it out on my own. I doubted it could be all that different from the fishing I'd done all summer in Alaska for salmon and trout. I needed that guide money to get me back to Colorado and I still had a long way to go.

After the call, I took a shower that seemed to last for an hour. I'd had the same set of drawers on for three days. When I finally walked out of the place and headed downtown to the fly shop, I felt like a new man.

The town of Smithers is idyllic, a caricature of a mountain town, clean and neat as a pin, its alpine themed architecture seems almost too cute for its own good, the kind of place a tourist would love. I found the shop down on Main Street and bought enough flies to warrant the amount of fishing intel that normally comes with that level of purchase. There's some fish in— in the Bulkley that runs right through town, I could try that. The Babine, where I really wanted to fish, was a bit of a drive, best wait for tomorrow when you have more time and can get an earlier start. I walked out of the shop with some flies that I really didn't need, but I had a good map out to the Babine River. I decided I'd give the Bulkley a go for now, since the better part of the day had already gotten away from me.

I spent about an hour swinging flies through what I considered likely holding water for steelhead with nary a touch. What the hell did I know about these fish anyway, other than what I read in some magazine? Apparently, not enough. Hooking one of these elusive fish in the first hour, on your first time out, was an unrealistic expectation in the first place; there's guys that fish for them nonstop for days without so much as a grab. They're a different breed of fishermen, those steelheaders, with the patience of Job.

I couldn't get excited about this fishing in town business either; maybe I'd been out in the wild too long. I've never enjoyed fishing next to too much civilization, it just didn't seem right somehow, like it didn't do the sport justice, sacrilegious in some sort of way. It reminded me of fishing the Blue River in Silverthorne, or the Animas through Durango. Fly fishing is a lot about aesthetics, being able to see the Gap parking lot in your backcast, doesn't really add much to that.

The only other fisherman I saw that afternoon hooked a bright silver torpedo that came flying out of the water in a long slick just below a big riffle in the bend three hundred yards above me. It could have been a steelhead or perhaps a coho, the Bulkley has both. It should have bolstered my hope, but it didn't. The bed back at the motel kept calling my name. Those last two nights cramped up on two tiny bucket seats with the center console gouging my ribs had taken its toll. The thought of a mattress, sheets, and a pillow after five months of not even seeing a bed were too much to resist. I drove back into town and ate a burger the size of Texas. I was asleep before it was even dark.

I woke up the next morning just before daylight, in the same position I'd fallen asleep in the night before. The sun came up on a quintessential fall day in the Canadian Rockies, azure sky with gold and red leaves on a backdrop of evergreens and snow in the distance, a slight chill in the morning air, but promise of warmth. The drive out to the Babine River was nothing but bright sunshine and beautiful scenery. I felt like a kid in a candy store.

When I turned off of the forest service road into the small parking lot next to a one lane wooden bridge, I was the only car there. The first thing I noticed was a makeshift cardboard sign tacked to a tree, with crude lettering in magic marker—Caution, mother and grizzly cubs seen in parking lot. The date on the sign was yesterday's. Shit. At this point, I didn't know whether to wind my watch or scratch my ass, so I read it again, hoping somehow I'd misinterpreted the only language I know how to read, write, and speak. The message hadn't changed since the first time I'd read it. I looked around for a while, but I didn't see any bears. I didn't think to look for tracks to substantiate the message of the sign; I took whoever had written those words as speaking the gospel truth. The thought did enter my mind for a moment that perhaps it was some cruel attempt at Canadian humor or an attempt to dissuade other fishermen from someone's favorite spot, but then I thought about all the bears I'd seen over the last three days and I knew it was, more than likely, legit.

I started fishing on the side of the river that bordered the road, with the Jeep and the parking lot still in plain view. I wasn't quite sure what my plan was, but after a while I realized it was ridiculous to think I could outrun a bear, whether it was for 500 yards, or a mile; besides, I wasn't happy with the spot I'd chosen since the water seemed too deep and slow to actually hold fish. After staring at it for a while, the other side of the river looked like better water, the way it always does when you're fishing anywhere for the first time. I reeled in and headed across the bridge.

I wasn't too long into it when I started catching fish—rainbows, pretty ones, not steelhead which are actually an anadromous form of rainbow, but fish nonetheless, and I had the place all to myself. I worked all the water that was still within sight of the parking lot, stripping streamers and skating big greased up sculpins, catching fish on both, and as my confidence increased, my anxiety over the bear situation seemed to dispel a bit. I moved around the bend ahead, happy to be catching anything at all, but still hoping to have a shot at the big steelhead I'd driven here for.

Once I was around the bend, the parking lot faded from view and the tree line closed in, down to the edge of the water. I saw a couple of spawned out salmon swimming in the back eddy there— lethargic, fungus covered, bear bait. The willies hit me again and I could feel the whole place closing in on me, out here in the wide-open nowhere. I couldn't take that forest closing in at my back; I waded out towards the middle and caught a few more fish on my way and stepped up onto the only rock that was out of the water. I stood there and took in the largess of the wilderness, a castaway on an island big enough for only my own two feet, and I came undone out there in the middle of that beautiful river, undone like never before, by loneliness. I did not want to disappear without a trace; I did not want to die alone. This place was too much for me, too big, too desolate. I couldn't handle it on my own.

I walked back to the parking lot and hurriedly changed out of my waders, leaving a splendid fall afternoon with hours of daylight remaining and a possible fish of a lifetime, behind. Fishing is my passion, but I never questioned that decision as I headed south out of Smithers, B.C., straight for Colorado.

Days later, I was forty-five minutes from Durango, the place I'd called home for over ten years, but I wasn't ready to drive back into town just yet. I'd been too long in the wild; I didn't know how I would assimilate. I didn't have a job or a place to live anymore; I'd left all that behind for Alaska. The Jeep needed new tires and I was damn near broke. I rolled out my sleeping bag and listened to the sound of the waterfall down in the canyon of Cascade Creek— nature's lullaby. I wasn't the least bit worried; I closed my eyes and knew that everything was bound to work out somehow.

Reflections from Dust

Jay Walden

5 REFLECTIONS FROM DUST

The day had started out with such promise; there were flapjacks, fried eggs, and homemade sausage, but now the ice cream had all turned to shit. He bent over, grasping at the loose fabric of his faded BDUs just above the knees— with such fervor that his knuckles were white. As he shrugged his shoulders to shift the weight of the pack higher onto his back, his chest heaved inadvertently, drawing in big mouthfuls of clear, mountain air that now came in gasps down to the deepest lobes of his lungs where they ached and burned. Stretching his neck and lifting his head toward the trail, he looked to the top that was still a quarter-mile away and a bead of sweat slowly rolled down the bridge of his nose; pausing temporarily at the tip, until it dropped off onto the ochre, talc dust covering his boots— spattering the tops, like tiny droplets of blood.

He thought of the sangre of Christ mixed with the tears of angels and figured this had to be just as painful. Just now, he thought of the sound of steel guitars and the shuffle of boots on sawdust, on an old creaking wood floor. He thought of cold beer and dancing a two-step to an old Bob Wills' song, his runner-up rodeo belt buckle rubbing against the buckle of some pretty young thing. He tried to think of anything except the hill before him and the two more miles before the trail ended. He stayed there, bent over and motionless, still clutching at the legs of his pants, with his mind now void and empty. It was like a pickle jar that had been used up, washed and rinsed, now waiting to be filled with assorted nuts, bolts, and washers of various, and assorted sizes.

None of this would have happened if his partner, Vern, had shown up. Vern had gone home last night for the pack mules and should have been back at first light. Cathy, his wife, had called at six this morning to say he wouldn't make it; he'd been back and forth to the toilet all night, done in by a liverwurst sandwich he'd been carrying around in his pack for the past two days. Things like this couldn't be helped— he guessed; but it sure left him in a lurch with an elk already quartered up in the woods.

He'd done the only thing he knew to do and called the boys who worked for him at the shop. They'd made it to the trailhead by 9:30, all of them standing there with their boots and backpacks on. Gallegos, Chavez, and Martinez—FEMA, he called them (Find-Every- Mexican- Available) young bucks full of piss and vinegar. Now they were all standing at the top of the hill, their packs loaded with an elk quarter each, looking down at him below; no doubt wondering, if he was going to make it.

With renewed determination, he wiped his mouth with the back of a hand that felt just like sandpaper, and stared down into the dust and spat, the dry spittle scattering in the wind like little pieces of Styrofoam. The sun was straight up overhead and it was hot. He shucked the load of the quarter he was carrying further up his back, and cinched down the waist belt of the pack. By God, he was going to do it; he'd done it plenty of times before, older now, or not. He'd do it if it wrenched his guts out and he died right here on the trail and someone didn't find his emaciated corpse until next season.

He looked again at the young men at the top that were staring down in his direction; behind him, he could hear the raucous arguments of the crows and magpies as they fought over the rights to the carcass and the offal of the elk. He wondered what the boys were discussing; perhaps they were thinking about leaving him here with a fire to ward off the predators like old Koskoosh in Jack London's *The Law of Life*. Maybe they wouldn't even waste the time with a fire, just leave him out here for the animals and elements like a Tibetan air burial. He straightened himself slowly and arched his back, stretching his aching muscles and put one foot forward, never looking up from the ground.

That was the way to do it; never look further than two or three feet ahead, focus on the next step, never look at the top while you were walking; it would always look too far and would kill your spirit. At this stage of his life, every step forward always seemed to leave more things behind; the very thought of it evaded him like the concept of long division.

When he had finally reached the top, he placed his back to a boulder and eased the pack onto it. He undid the buckle at the waist, slipped his arms out and the pack rolled over with a thud. His shirt was soaked and the wind rising on the thermals from the valley floor below was scented with Ponderosa pine, dust, and the musty smell of elk, and he felt its coolness like air-conditioning. He was sitting now, and the young men were all standing in the shade of the big pines as he stripped to his t-shirt that was drying in concentric, salt-rimed circles, where it clung to his body.

Chavez spoke first, "Why do you hunt in this God-forsaken country in the first place? It's the only place I've ever been where it's uphill, coming and going."

He took them all in as a group, like trying to paint them with his eyes from a picture that wouldn't quite come into focus.

"Well, for one thing, nobody else hunts back here. And for another, I know the country— know where the elk are."

When he had finished, Martinez spoke up, "If you ever kill another one, just don't call us. There was laughter in his voice just at the end, but also a note of sincerity; or sarcasm. It was difficult to distinguish between the two.

Unwilling to be left out, Gallegos looked directly at him and took his turn, "When you have to tie an animal to a tree to keep it from sliding over the mountain while you field dress it, maybe it's time to rethink your choices."

He looked again at the group, feeling slightly embarrassed about the whole matter and a quizzical look came over his face like a man that needed to scratch his ass in public, but didn't quite know how to go about it. Shaking his head, he slipped his arms back through the straps and wrestled it onto his back, rising from a squat, like a weight-lifter going for some type of medal.

"Well boys, this ain't buying the baby any new dress. Let's get this sum-bitch down the mountain."

They turned and formed single-file with him in the rear, and headed through the trees, deeper into the darkness of the quiet shade.

The trail was now flat before them as it clung to the side of the mountain, just below where the tree line stopped. He stared ahead at the backs of the boys and at the tops of the canvas game bags; where the quarters that had been trimmed at the shank of the legs protruded from their packs. Unless you are the lead dog, the view never changes. He could feel the heavy weight as it pulled and strained at his neck and shoulders. The young men in front walked effortlessly, as if the burden they carried did not exist, somehow denying the laws of gravity; and, the whole element of the thing struck him as decidedly unfair. The young men would forget this. This would soon become nothing to them; there would be other, more important thoughts, to occupy their minds. There would be girls to break their hearts, marriage; perhaps, someday— mortgages, career selections, children, possibly even divorce; important life decisions that would occupy their time and consideration. They would forget this, but he would not. He was tangled up in the disparity of all the priorities that come with age, where sometimes day to day survival came as heavy as the dead weight upon his back.

He thought of all of the people that had loved him at one time and wondered where they had gone now. Unlike these young men which still had the best years of their life ahead, the dead and dying think of no one but themselves; which was their earned right. The toes of his boots stubbed against the rocks in the trail and he consciously made an effort to lift his feet higher to avoid them. There was only a half of mile left now until the trail turned sharply down the mountain; the worst part was over.

When it came, it came like a sudden flash of lightening, with the deepest of cobalt— silver-blue-white, and metallic— like the ice that climbers seek in the coldest part of winter in which to sink their adzes— the kind they know to be honest, the kind they know that will carry the weight. As he came to, he was sitting with his torso in the oak brush, his head hanging downward toward legs that were splayed in the dust of the trail like a piece of kindling that had not been entirely split in two. He could hear noise that sounded like voices, fathomless noise, reverberating inside the hollow of his head. Someone was splashing water on his face and he felt a hand on his back, struggling with the pack and he could feel a wave of nausea sweeping over him that was as ugly as congealed grease in a skillet, as ugly as a negative bank balance, ugly, ugly to the bone. He wondered if he was dying and he could feel everything fading from himself, and it wasn't so bad. It wasn't so bad, he thought; dying was just like living and you did it effortlessly.

He would never see the note— the note that Judy had written to say that she was on her way to meet the ladies for her weekly Canasta get-together. The note that said he was welcome back to hunt again next year and that she had enjoyed his stay at the cabin. He would never see the note that would eventually find its way into the trash with all the wet coffee grounds, wadded paper towels, and the leftover crusts from the toast that someone didn't like; the note that would be among the remainder of the egg whites that you could never quite completely remove from the shell and would blur the ink into intelligible gibberish. None of it mattered now anyway.

The wind picked up and he could hear it as it moved through the tops of the tall trees near the crest of the ridge, mixing with the sound of shuffling of boots in the dust beside him. He thought that he could smell moisture in the air and he wondered if it was going to rain. He mumbled something and the three young men bent closer to hear it again, as it came out in a whisper.

"Play something beautiful for me," he said; and he opened his eyes into brilliant, white light that none of them could see.

Between Seasons

Jay Walden

6 BETWEEN SEASONS

Pre-dawn darkness, it's bitter cold as I step outside to start the car— defroster on high, to melt the thick ice on the windshield while I load my bags and do one last look around. A ragged plastic shopping bag rattles in a ragged wind; stuck in the chain link fence, shredded beyond any real recognition. Dirty snow in a patchwork, where winter sun can't reach—trees, plants, and grass, all brown and gray, blend with the dirt and frozen mud into one lifeless, dull collage that looks as if it has drawn its last breath. An angel fallen from grace, unrepentant; I am through with winter.

Six-and-one-half hours later, I'm sitting at C-13 in DFW awaiting the plane that will take me to Miami, then beyond.

Four a.m. wake up call from the front desk and now the alarm clock goes off; as well. Simple pandemonium temporarily ensues. I handle each intrusion, one at a time, like fighting two fires that have broken out simultaneously; answering the phone first, listening to the first part of the recorded message, and hang up. I can't find my glasses to read the instructions for turning off the vexatious alarm. I stumble to the bathroom, groping at the walls like a blind man and flip on the light switch, and find them there on the sink. Back to the clock; I've got it— silence, then peace.

I press the button on the coffeemaker that I prepped before I went to bed at midnight, it gurgles and the water I must have spilled on the warmer plate sizzles, then pops like popcorn. I chug the first cup, with the thought that I didn't get enough sleep, knowing that I'm now just going to have to suck it up for the remainder of the day. I hope that coffee and adrenaline will be enough. I open the sliding glass door to the patio and notice that the wind has picked up during the night, blowing straight onshore. I can hear the breakers; booming, colliding with the reef in the distance.

Forty-five minutes to the marina. The GPS tells me to turn right in 250 feet, in that authoritative type of female voice I've conditioned myself to avoid over so many years. There are metal gates just like in the directions I received from the guide service yesterday, but it doesn't look right. I ignore the command and skip the turn, and go over the bridge— apparently the same bridge that is supposed to indicate I've gone too far. The GPS tells me to take the next right and turn around. There is a lot of traffic on this skinny, winding road, for six a.m. and everyone seems to be driving way too fast. I acquiesce to the superiority of technology and take the next right like I am told this time. I am on a side-street following commands from some lady I don't even know.

It's getting lighter. I can see my surroundings a bit now and I'm smack-dab in the middle of some spooky looking barrio. I wind through narrow one-way streets following turn by turn directions— stray dogs roam the streets, overflowing garbage cans, cars up on blocks, detritus of life; a rooster crows, then another, a plane overhead landing with mas turistas, like myself. All of this seems too close to the kind of fish I hope to catch today. At the point where I think I will never make it out of this labyrinth, I am back to the main highway that I just left. I turn and head back for 500 yards to the turn-off I originally passed on, and announce myself to the guard at the gate.

I park the car and grab my sling pack that contains my bug spray, sunscreen, sandwich, and a granola bar—the guide's supposed to have water. A young girl is cleaning the deck of a boat with a mop and says good morning in Spanish. I ask her if she knows where slip 79 is and she points down the dock.

In the half-light of a beginning sunrise and the incandescent glow of the light over the slip, I see my guide sitting on a storage locker at the edge of the wooden walkway. He's in his 30's; I would guess— unshaven, wearing a pair of thin windpants, long sleeved UV t-shit, flip flops, and a grimy ball cap. He looks like he has had a hard night, or a hard week. I am impressed and take heart; he looks like every other guide I have ever known.

"Are you Randy?"

"I sure am."

That accent, was that Brooklyn,? takes me off guard.

He seems moody, sullen— that's o.k., it's early. All the best guides I know are moody; I think it comes with the occupation— dealing with too many strangers, having to always get up at God-awful hours.

We back out of the slip and the boat chugs through the no wake zone and he addresses another guide in the next slip over, in perfect Spanish. He tells me we'll probably get into some fish today, but to just remember that it's called fishing not catching, a guide-speak cliché that is designed to be a disclaimer, if things get ugly out there. His attempts at lowering my expectations are lost and I am undeterred, as he brings the boat up on plane and scatters a flock of snowy egrets among the mangroves, in a rising sun.

Five hookups and three fish to the boat, along with a few small snook. It's turning out to be a very good day. I work the edge of the mangrove again to a large head and fin I saw roll earlier. My fly is swimming around down there in 18 inch strips, its beady eyes cast about for a one-hundred-pound predator with a mouth the size of a bushel basket— my fly, with its butt puckered up, is hoping he makes it through the gauntlet. Four feet from the bank there is a hard tug and a splash, and the slack line at my feet is taken up in an instant. I instinctively point the rod toward the commotion that has now moved off 20 yards in the blink of an eye, like I've been doing this all my life. The fly line slices through the water with the sound of a giant sheet of paper being torn in half. The reel screams as a silver missile breaches the surface and falls five feet from where it first broke the water. I point the rod and bow, like I am supposed to do; the reel screams again as the fish makes an arc towards more open water.

"That's a better fish than the others," Randy says.

I know it, but I don't say anything; I'm too busy concentrating on the job at hand. This fish will probably go 50 pounds, maybe 60. I want to catch this one; I don't want to screw this up.

Out of the corner of my eye, I see Randy head back toward the middle of the boat for both of our cell phones. He wants to be ready for a picture when it happens. No time to be fooling around for a camera when you have a fish like this alongside the boat, we'll both have our hands full; it'll take all we've got, working together, to land this fish.

I can feel it coming— another jump— and I ready myself. Another sudden burst of speed and he's airborne again. I point the rod and bow, and handle it perfectly. As he lands, I still feel his weight and I know I've survived the jump. Then, slack.

Randy, with his back to me, turns and sees me reeling up the slack line.

"What happened?"

"Hook came out."

It's a meager explanation, but fully sums up the

scenario. There is nothing else left to say about the matter.

"Well, you didn't do anything wrong. It just happens sometimes."

I am not consoled, but I'm not heartbroken, either. I know that, "It just happens, sometimes."

It's getting hot. I look at my watch; it's almost time for our trip to end. I finish reeling up and stow the rod and Randy pulls up the anchor, tossing weeds that cling to the rope back into the water.

The boat comes up on plane through the lagoon, the spray and the wind feel good— refreshing, and I forget about my tiredness and my lack of sleep for a moment. I stand next to Randy so we can talk without shouting. He's not grumpy anymore; talkative, actually. He tells me about moving down here from New York with his parents when he was seven, which explains his Spanish, without me asking. I ask him if he's caught any big fish recently, and he mentions a seventy pounder that he boated last week.

"I really don't remember those fish too much; the ones I lose, are actually the ones that really stick with me."

That's right Randy—I think it, but don't say it, while a video clicks on in my head of a huge brown trout I lost at the net on the Taylor River in Colorado; a trophy bull elk I missed during a downpour of sleet in October; a tom turkey with a beard dragging the ground; women; friends and family; the list goes on with vivid effectuation and clarity like it all happened yesterday. It's the ones you lose that really stick with you. It is one of the few things I know to be absolutely true about life. Margaritas, mofongo and red snapper with creole sauce tonight, will help to temporarily dim my memory of that final jump from that last fish, but I know that same scene could be my last thought, my last lucid reflection, should I live to be an old man.

I hand the keys to the valet, who wants to talk fishing and asks how my trip went. I'm too tired for a stop-and-chat, so I just say, "Great," and give him a thumbs up, and head for the lobby. I look a Ralph Steadman caricature of myself—slightly hung-over, sunburned, sleep deprived, hungry, and disheveled, all rolled into the same package.

I head straight for the beach and she's down at the far end of all the other chairs, where it's quieter, reading. Her tan is coming along nicely. There's another empty recliner waiting there for me with a towel already stretched out—of all the people I have ever known, she is the most considerate and thoughtful.

"How'd it go?"

I hand her my phone and she scrolls through the pictures.

"Oh, my. Those are some big fish."

I high-five her and give her a kiss, then peel off my shirt and shoes, and fall face-first onto the lounge. I can feel the sun; warm on my back, legs, and soles of my feet, as I listen to the cycle of waves coming, and then going, from the shore. I reach across and hold her hand until mine drifts lifelessly into the sand and I drool onto the beach towel.

Three days later, I'm staring through a small, scratched plexiglass window at a long set of islands surrounded by miles of turquoise flats and sugary white beaches. There is a blue that I have no words for, where the water drops off into the deep. It'll be twenty degrees at home when I finally step off the plane tonight, after the last leg of this trip—still mid-February. The dry fly fishing won't get good until the first or second week of May. I'd like to un-do the latch on the emergency door and sail outside, D.B. Cooper-style with nothing but my rod tube in my hands, wade the flats down there for a couple months until things warm a bit up north, live on coconuts, conch, and lobster, but I slept through the demo on how to open the damn thing. I wonder if my mental condition qualifies for the type of emergency the flight attendants discussed in my absence.

I look again at the turquoise flats, wondering if I can see a bonefish tailing, the tip-up of a permit on a crab, the gulp of a tarpon, which is absurd at this altitude. The cabin is filled with that strange noise of commercial aircraft, like the 60 cycle hum of an amp, rendering everything else silent, except for the whistling of the wind over the wings; elusive, like so many things I find harder to hold on to as I grow older.

Cansado y Viejo

Jay Walden

7 CANSADO Y VIEJO

Everyone said Carl Thompson lived life on his own terms. Carl always liked that depiction of himself, although he knew he had enough skeletons in his closet to fill an average graveyard, just like anyone else. He'd worked hard since he had gotten a little older to keep his life simpler, and outside of his love for good bourbon, fly fishing, and Stilton cheese, he didn't carry a lot of bad habits or baggage. Carl generally avoided town, but today was going to be an exception. The doctor's office was becoming an inherent evil that couldn't be avoided to address one nagging malady or another that went hand- in- hand with age, and lately it appeared that the devil was always getting was his due.

This latest visit really didn't give him much to go on. Outside of Doc Lyons' last comment, that seemed like more of an afterthought now, "And you should stop drinking— altogether," there wasn't much advice at all. At least there would be no pills this time. He hated the damn pills, mostly hated trying to keep up with them— which ones to take before bed; which ones to take with food; which ones to take without. It made him tired just thinking about it; and his thinking could get messed up when he was tired. The drinking issue would have to be worked over later— right now he was played out and he didn't trust his judgment when he felt that way.

It was still early, but Carl already felt like the day was washed up. The doctor visit had thrown a monkey wrench into his daily routine that otherwise held no big plans, and the whole thing was an inconvenience that he would have preferred to avoid from the get go. Determined to salvage what was left of the morning, he turned left onto Main Street for coffee and inspiration, parking on the shaded side of the street where the facades of the store fronts still subdued a better part of the morning sun. He rummaged in the console for change and came up with a quarter and a dime— it would be enough; he didn't plan to stay that long.

He'd always thought that the parking ought to be free anyway. If you were from out-of-state and ran over on the meter, they gave you a pass, just put a little warning under your wiper that said, "Howdy Partner," and reminded you to pay next time. If you had in-state plates, you got a ticket, without fail. It just wasn't right. It was a small thing; but his whole life was a series of small victories and small joys— and pain crammed in there where it would fit; and he could see no reason why the parking issue should be any different. Anyway, it was a damn shame that the rest of the city government couldn't operate half as efficiently as the parking enforcement division. They were on you like white on rice the minute your time ran out.

After feeding the meter, he headed up the sidewalk and passed the coffeehouse with all the bicycles and benches out front. He'd been in there a couple of times with Tuley's teenage grandson, but he didn't feel like going in there today. He needed a quieter place, since there were so many new things rolling around in his head like rocks in a tumbler. There really wasn't anything wrong with the coffeehouse— they had good coffee in there— but it was a busy place, too busy for today and his present mood.

The diner would be a better choice; besides, he didn't like drinking his coffee out of a paper cup if he didn't have to, no matter how good it was. Up at the diner, they served their coffee in those heavy ceramic mugs that came up to your mouth with enough heft and effort so that you felt you were accomplishing something; a mug that you could wrap your fingers around and warm your hands in the wintertime, not some paper cup you had to leave on the table, waiting for it to cool before you could pick it up. By the time you got to the bottom, that coffee was always cold. And then there was the pie; everyone knew about the pie— homemade apple with sharp cheddar melted on top, always came that way whether you'd specified it or not. He wondered who'd come up with such a strange concoction; whoever it was had been a genius, no doubt. For Carl, it ranked right up there with the invention of the wheel and Gutenberg's printing press, and rivaled the Great Wall of China.

If familiarity bred contempt, it hadn't done so in his feelings for the diner. With the exception of some tattered, laminated menus that were occasionally smudged with egg yolk like some page in a scratch and sniff book, the place was neat and clean. Mostly, it was a quiet repose where old ranchers liked to hold court over chicken fried steak and bottomless cups of coffee, and college kids came to nurse their hangovers— a sort of throwback to another time when things didn't move so quickly. Carl knew it as a good place to come to and get your head on straight.

These infrequent visits to town still served to protect his anonymity and he guessed that he could drop over dead in here and no one would know his name without checking his wallet first. He liked being alone anyway, or at least he didn't mind it anymore. He couldn't remember when he first started feeling that way, but he was sure it had been a long time ago. Tuley came along now and again, if he thought he wouldn't have to pay. Tuley was tighter than Uncle Dick's hatband and didn't care who knew it either— kind of proud of it in a way— never could enjoy life because he spent it waiting around for the other shoe to drop; figured there was only so much to go around in this world and he wouldn't get his share if someone else got theirs first, which was an awful way for a man to feel after 67 years of living.

Outside of a few more locals, the place was quiet. You could always count on the handful of retirees that had been up since four in the morning, exercising their God given right to spend their Social Security checks how they damn well pleased, and free, senior citizen refills. They were always the first ones in the door and headed to their favorite booths as the lights were turned on at six. The vacation crowd wouldn't start filtering in until later, seemingly flaunting their idleness to the rest of the patrons that they had no particular place to be and all the time in the world to get there. Carl was glad for the solitude, for whatever the reason, because he seemed to focus better in the quiet. Maybe he was selfish for wanting this time alone, but the last thing he needed was to be spotted by a tableful of tourists with a bunch of noisy kids, asking about local attractions and driving directions. He took a seat up near the front and nodded at the waitress when she caught his eye and lifted the coffee pot in her hand. Satisfied that he had fulfilled his end of the nonverbal communication between them, he broke eye contact and sat staring out the plate glass window, and somewhere between a totally empty head— and the thought that there was a big difference between how you figured your life was going to turn out— and how it actually did, his coffee appeared. He sipped it slowly, recalling a line from Hemingway's *The Sun Also Rises,* that, "Caffeine puts a man on her horse and a woman in her grave." He couldn't remember which character had said it, and the gender switch was an amorphism that Carl could never quite get a handle on, but he liked the quote anyway. He smiled and put his cup back down onto the table, replaying the quote in his head and thinking that he could sure use that horse today.

The fact that he'd remembered the quote at all gave him hope that at least his mind wasn't going on him too; something that he'd begun to worry about lately, when he'd catch himself staring off into space, thinking about things that he hadn't considered for such a long time. Nowadays, he was always lost in the kind of thoughts he never wanted to share, the kind that always led to those outcomes you couldn't undo and ended up haunting you for the rest of your life. Since the years that remained were far less than those behind, time seemed too far removed to worry about them anyway, and he figured you could handle about anything in life, except regret. Realizing regret at this late hour in life never did anybody any good, and really there was no recompense for things lost without a grasp of proper penitence to help reclaim them, so the whole exercise was probably a big waste of his time. For the most part, he was never sure if it was better to reckon with such things or just let them go, and he became preoccupied with that argument, unaware of how much time had passed. Looking down into his near- empty cup, the man in the bottom stared back with a momentary sense of clarity and he decided he'd better make a move before the caffeine wore off and his thoughts became muddled again, so he picked up the check and headed towards the cash register.

The help here wasn't overly friendly—efficient was probably a better description, although they usually managed a smile when it came to the taking your money part. At the other place down the street, all their help were pretty, young hippy girls from the local college, always tanned and wearing sundresses in the summertime. Carl had known girls like that, growing up, girls that didn't need makeup to enhance their looks, girls that were just naturally beautiful. He left his change with the cashier and pushed through the heavy glass door, and out into a morning sun that had filled the street like soft, warm butter. He shook his head and wondered about himself. A man his age had no business thinking about such things, no business at all. He wondered how thoughts like that ever got into a man's head in the first place.

By the time he got back home it was already approaching noon. He turned on the water in the kitchen sink to wash this morning's breakfast dishes, which triggered an overwhelming urge to pee again. BPH, his doctor called it, more like BPA, he thought, because it's always a big pain in the ass. But, it was something he was growing accustomed to with age, just like the other unpleasantries of growing older, like having hair grow everywhere it was not supposed to and not in the places it should, the youthful fire in your belly now replaced by acid reflux, or insomnia that left you fearing the bed rather than the monsters beneath it, as when you were younger— bothersome and annoying things that made life more difficult— but not things that were going to break you, unless maybe they all piled on you at once.

After he had put away the dishes, he grabbed the rod tube with his favorite three-weight from the corner of the spare bedroom. On his way out, he picked up the wader bag with the rest of his fishing gear and headed outside to the truck. The camping equipment and everything he would need were already under the camper shell where he always kept them. He'd make a couple of sandwiches and stop along the way for a block of ice for the cooler, and he was set.

Headed back up Main Street and out of town, he

drove mindlessly, only noting whether the lights were red or green and an occasional pedestrian in the crosswalk. The distraction of the shops and the sidewalk traffic became a blur that never fully engaged his brain. His mind was already on the mountains and you only needed half a mind to drive, any dimwit with a driver's license could tell you that. A few weeks from now these distractions of cars and tourists would be gone anyway. There would be no more "Howdy Partners" until the snow was deep and the skiers arrived.

Five miles up the canyon, they were working on the road again and a disinterested flagger that looked like he was reconsidering his career choice, had a line of traffic stopped. Attempting to make the best of the delay, Carl rolled down the window and turned off the engine, the sights and sounds turning his half-hearted ambivalence to eager anticipation. Out of the passenger side, he could see the white crests of the stream as the water licked against the boulders, and the tops of the green grass that lined its banks, dotted here and there with the blue of columbine and red Indian paintbrush. Through the lodgepole that stood between the highway and the stream, he could hear the sound of moving water as it met its resistance against stone— liquid life, alive, rising and falling in cadence with the breeze. He felt the coolness of the air as it moved through the shade of the pine, its perfumed scent of pitch, bark, and needle, resplendent, and unmistakably clean. He closed his eyes and tried to capture it in his head, a requiem that lingered, but would not stay; instead it slowly slipped away, the way joy in life can at times, little by little, like the fading of a favorite garment over time.

Startled from his daydream, the movement of vehicles in the other lane brought him back around to the reality of the moment. Rubbing his hand down his face to help clear his head, he started the engine, put the truck in gear and waited for his line of traffic to move, glad that he didn't have much farther to drive.

When he reached the familiar pull-out upriver, he was out of the truck and headed toward the overlook in a trot, before the dust had settled. Across the river, where a steep avalanche chute ended at the water's edge, he could see the whisp-like images of delicate insects highlighted in the early afternoon sun against the boulders, their angelic, translucent wings bobbing and dipping like graceful debutantes at a Southern cotillion. From time to time a fish would rise; framing a dimple on the water's surface, then carried downstream, until it was lost in the current. Pale Morning Duns, he whispered under his breath, wondering if perhaps it was possible to wish for something powerfully enough to will it to happen, but deep down, doubting that the world really worked that way.

His head was buzzing like a bee inside and he felt with certainty that he could have stayed there for hours, transfixed with the magic, but he knew that he had business to attend to. Hustling back to the truck, he dropped the tailgate and began grabbing gear as fast as his hands would work— wool socks, waders, boots, and shirt, tossed on like a fireman responding to a four-alarm fire. In no time at all he was jointing the three-piece rod together, sighting down the guides

to line them up, and twisting the nut on the reel seat
to lock in the reel. He grabbed the box that contained
his dry flies and stuffed it into his shirt pocket,
slammed the tailgate shut, then doubled over the
thick end of his leader, stringing it through the guides
as he walked.

At the water's edge, Carl could already feel beads of
sweat forming and channeling down his back. He did
not mind it; instead, welcoming the warmth of the
sun on his neck, knowing all too soon that it would
be gone, replaced by an autumn with the brevity of a
cool wind passing down the canyon, and shortly— all
of this, taken by the gray, cruel loneliness of winter.
Summer always seemed too short, and the
inevitability of winter, which he did not like, always
seemed to rob too much of its glory. He was the only
person he knew that could stand in ninety-degree heat
and dread the snow.

Unwrapping several loops from his tippet spool, he
clipped off a piece and put on his glasses to tie the
knot to his leader. As he crossed the monofilaments
to begin the knot, his eyes would not focus on the
line; seeing instead, pale, dry hands, with bones
gnarled and withered like branches in winter, hands
that no longer belonged to him, hands of a stranger
with skin of dusty parchment, thin, and dotted with
age. The image unnerved him and he turned his head
to avoid it, drawing a deep breath and closing his eyes
to banish the unwelcome visage that had burned into
his brain. After a moment, he gazed across the pool,
the ephemeral shapes of the mayflies and rise rings,
restoring his senses. Jesus, I'm a sight for sore eyes,
he said aloud, fully aware that there was no one else

to hear him.

Finishing the knot, Carl tied on the small Comparadun, carefully clipping off the tag end of the tippet. He peeled off some line from the reel and measured the distance to the last rise with a single false cast. The familiar swish of the line through the guides brought pleasure to him, its rhythmic slice through the medium of air, a comfort that had managed to keep him firmly connected to terra-firma, for the larger part of his living days.

After a splendid afternoon, taking four good fish and a few smaller ones in the pool just below the bridge, he did not want the day to end. There were still several hours of good light and it would be a shame to waste them while the weather was so pleasant and these fish so willing to come to the fly. He reeled in the slack line and placed the fly in the hook-keeper, and started back up the hill toward the bridge.

When he had crossed the river and began to walk down the opposite bank, the growling in his stomach reminded him of the sandwich in his waistpack. Halfway down the narrow trail, he sat among the boulders of the abutment, where he could still see the water and the fish below. Removing the sandwich, he unwrapped it and sat there in the quiet, alone, and not afraid to be alone, silently eating with small, deliberate bites and drinking the cold, clear water from his water bottle. When he was finished, he wandered among the boulders and filled both hands with raspberries that were growing among the wild roses still in bloom. Returning to his previous spot, he sat again, eating the berries and watching the flow of the water, content, and in no particular hurry to fish, although he could still see the splashy rises along the edges of the stream. It felt good to be on this boulder in the sun, good to be among the roses and the berries, and good to be with this river and these fish, with this big earth turning, spinning, and breathing in and out, its great sighs of relief.

Gathering himself, he walked the remaining distance to the water and waded out to clear his backcast from the bank. An hour later, he had brought four more fish to the net, a regard rising up in him to near contentment. Of the many things in life; at least this is one he did well, and he supposed that accounted for something.

From that other world, up where fish, sky and the tops of tall conifer all meld, a distant rumble of thunder came by surprise and he looked up in amazement at the disappearing thin slice of blue, high above the walls of the canyon. Knowing enough about summer thunderstorms in the mountains, he scrambled into his pack and by the time he had retrieved his jacket, the first raindrops had begun to fall. An immediate flash of lightening and a whip-crack of thunder suddenly snapped his head skyward to a dark band of clouds that hung over the north rim of the valley, like a pall. Upriver, he could see the large raindrops moving toward him, turning the surface of the water to a boil as it came. He ran for the truck as it overtook him, overcome by a wall of water, followed by pea-sized hail. As he swung into the cab of the truck; bringing rivulets from his rain jacket and waders into the seat— the hail ceased and the rain intensified, coming down in buckets and turning the windshield into an opaque waterfall. The rumbling of thunder, reverberating off the canyon walls like cannon fire, shook the ground beneath and focused his thoughts heavenward. A bible verse from his childhood, "Oh ye hypocrites, ye can discern the face of the sky; but can ye not discern the signs of the times?" stuck in his head like a broken record.

Feeling that the day was now lost, he waited in the truck another half-hour, anyway. The clouds had now banked into an ugly darkness that ran the length of the sky above, swallowing up the remaining light of the canyon, as a snake swallows a frog. Rolling down the window, he could feel the cold wind on his face, and he knew without doubt, that the day was now over, and that summer was gone with it.

On the short ride back to his old familiar campsite, all the positivity of the day seemed to have washed out of him. Even the warm, brown bark of the trees; now wet from the rain, had taken on a lurid, black countenance that suggested a foreboding of gloom that he could not dispel. Through the fog of the windshield, the river had transformed into a solid ribbon of gray slate with the life seemingly drained from it, its rain slickened boulders, ill-lighted, cold, and stoic, relocated from another planet. His only comfort came from the warmth of the truck's heater and the immutable shush of the heavy ply tires on the wet pavement, a sound as soothing and gentle as a mother quieting her child. As he pulled onto the two-track that led through the sodden, dripping ponderosas, the dampened carpet of wet needles muffled his arrival to a quiet, and he was overcome with loneliness, passing ever deeper into a darkening cathedral of pine.

Once the truck had found its own way to a level resting place beneath the trees, he turned off the engine, exited the cab, and took extra care to gently shut the door, surrendering himself to the quiet that covered the place like a cold, wet blanket. With the passing of the storm and evening approaching, the sky had lightened to a smoky gray, leaving only minutes to get things squared away before complete darkness fell. He raised the back window of the camper shell, lowered the tailgate, and took out a folding camp chair, looking all the while at his drenched jacket, waders, and boots, dreading the unpleasant task of removing them. Someone ought to start a mobile wader removal service for old, arthritic fishermen—probably make a fortune; he chuckled, hoping for comfort in the sound of his own voice, but his feeble attempt fell flat, like whistling past the graveyard.

He unzipped the jacket and peeled himself out of it, then slipped on his old, thick wool sweater he'd retrieved from the top of his backpack. The arms down near the cuffs were ragged and patched with rough stitching, done by an old girlfriend, years ago, now long gone. He remembered how proud she'd been of her work, always eager to please by doing the little things he generally neglected. He'd let that one slip away too, just like all the others and he didn't remember or care to recall the details anymore. Truth be known, Carl could screw up a wet dream when it came to dealing with women. He stared again at the old wool sweater with its ragged sleeves and the dried elk blood from last fall's hunt. That old sweater had character, and embraced him like a warm hug. If he ever got around to writing his last will and testament he was going to ask to be buried in it.

To steel himself from the unpleasant task of removing the waders and boots, he poured three fingers of Woodford Reserve into his blue, tin coffee cup. In the clean air he could smell the smoky, alcohol aroma of the whiskey as it flared his nostrils and resonated in the back of his throat, a redolence that always brought back memories of college football games, autumn leaves, and cute, drunk sorority girls, in a time so distant, it seemed like another life; and the thought of so many passing years made him sad. It was too much to wrap his mind around, so he let it go to wherever it was that such thoughts go, perhaps in the same place where all the missing socks from the dryer ended up. He didn't know how it worked for others, but for Carl, those joyless thoughts were never as far away as he would have liked them to be, always turning up, again and again, like a bad penny.

After changing into dry, warm clothes, he polished off the rest of the bourbon from the cup, its contents burning in his gut like the second circle of hell. Across the empty highway and below, he could hear the roar of the stream as it picked up speed through the steep canyon, and was drawn to it as ancient mariners were drawn to their deaths by a Siren's song, fueled by their daily rations of rum.

He refilled the tin cup, thinking of the doctor's warning earlier this morning. He should probably give it up. There were all kinds of personal stories of people that had done it, throwing otherwise, good, full bottles of booze into any number of creeks, rivers, and lakes, saying they'd never touch the stuff again. He doubted the veracity of such tales, having never found any of these bottles, despite his countless hours on the water. Well, we were all going to die of something eventually. There wasn't a single one of us that was ever going to get out of this world alive. He was willing to bet that most people's bad habits probably followed them to the grave. If you lived well and were lucky enough, you left them there, and that was the end of that, or so he hoped. He slipped on his Wellies from the back of the truck and walked toward the sound of the water.

Crossing the deserted highway, he followed the path onward toward the stream. The sky had cleared and the moon was out, reflecting raindrops on the grass like scattered blades of quicksilver. In the distance he could see the stream that now seemed to be a churning, dark, and angrier version of its former self. At the water's edge, he squatted and sat on his haunches, mesmerized by the din of the undulating sheet before him, its frothing, swirling surface, pounded white by the rocks below, it leadened underbelly, defying an alchemy that refused to be turned to gold.

Overcome by a strange compulsion to rise and wade forward from shallow to deep, he could feel in his mind the sensation, of first the sand, the rounded cobble beyond, and then the alluvial gravel of ancient glaciers, behind the boulders. Perhaps led by the hand of God, or the bourbon in his cup; he could not tell. There was surely no burning bush, no pillar of salt, so how did one know? Dreamlike, onward he moved, wading from the mud of the bank, then further, the sand moving beneath as each footfall disturbed the shifting bottom. Onward, as the cold gripped first his ankles, shins, then knees, his feet registering the changing of the structure below. Onward, with wanton desire to go where there was neither light nor sound, to where nothing was everything, dragging with him all the worst that life had to offer, its pain and suffering, guilt and regret, and all the petty, mundanity of it all; its disquieted weariness, smothered once and forever. Deeper, colder, he could feel the buoyancy of his body increasing as he went, until his steps became effortless and his body seemed to float— as if walking on air. Further along, until the current from the edge of the boulder grabbed him, pulling down his shoulders, and then his head, until the light of the world above was reduced and dancing on the head of a pin. The vivid effectuation haunted him as the light disappeared and he felt himself spinning, tossed like a lifeless ragdoll into the rolling, cold, raging darkness, downstream.

After a while he rose and stretched, and stared unblinkingly into the darkness, to the trees beyond the water. He was tired, bone tired, with all the life wrung out of him, and his head was heavy with the quiet disappointment of all that he had not become in life. He turned and headed back up the path, struck dumb that he had entertained the idea of wading into the stream. The stars, diamond studded against an ink black firmament of nothingness, made him feel small and seemed to compound the shame of his earlier thoughts.

Back at the campsite, he built a small fire for the

company of the flame and the light, and sat in his chair next to the fire ring as the shadows danced against the cold, wet, granite background, mocking his every move. After finishing the contents of the cup, he reflected on thoughts as ancient as fire itself and wondered how many men had done the same, since the eons of its discovery. The past was the past, he thought, and it was better to live in the moment, a phrase that tripped easily enough off the tongue, but few people in real life ever realized. Longing for sleep and a refuge from his thoughts, he kicked the dampened dirt over the fire and walked the short distance to the back of the truck. Once inside, he crawled into his heavy down sleeping bag and slept the sleep of kings.

In the morning when he awakened, the rain had washed the sky to a robin's egg blue, the kind of brilliant blue that hurt your eyes and came only with the arrival of autumn. He rinsed his cup from the night before and filled it with cold water from the cooler, then dumped in a spoonful and a half of instant coffee. He'd long since given up the practice of building a morning fire or dragging out the camp stove to heat his water and he'd developed a liking to drinking his coffee cold now on such occasions. Thick and dark, like 10-W30 after a 5,000 mile oil change, he could feel it breathing life back into his soul as he sipped it, sitting there on the tailgate.

When he had finished, he loaded the camp chair into the back of the truck with the lone thought that it was time to call the dogs and piss on the fire. Back in the cab of the truck, he twisted the key in the ignition and the engine turned over. Patsy Cline came on the radio as he pulled back onto the pavement. The road was now dry and the sun was out, and his head had cleared and he was a happier man for it. There were still plenty of reasons to go on—young girls in soft cotton dresses that still made an old man's heart beat a little faster, ripe raspberries for the enjoyment of both man and beast, late afternoons in the mountains with fish that still rose to the dry fly, good strong coffee in a heavy mug, apple pie with cheddar cheese melted on top; all of that, and memories of dark water— he knew there would always be the dark water.

Alpha and Omega

Jay Walden

8 ALPHA AND OMEGA

We were standing in the meat isle, looking at ribeyes, and I was explaining why the ones with a lot of marbling always taste better, when the priest walked up. They noticed each other instantly and both of them smiled as if on cue.

"Father Thomas, how have you been?" she said, with the smile coming through in her voice, sounding almost giddy, like she always did when she ran into someone she knew.

"Very well, thank you, and how about you? I haven't seen you at mass for a while."

Still no introduction and I was glad. I wanted to remain anonymous if possible, invisible would have been even better. I wanted to blend in with the meat there in the display, maybe down at the far end where the cow tongues and pigs feet were, where less people shopped—not up here with the ribeyes and filets. I could just walk away, though I'd arouse more suspicion. I decided to hold tight and let this one play out—hope for the best.

They were facing each other now; which was good, so it took me out of the picture a bit. I busied myself, picking up a couple of steaks, examining them like I was from the USDA and shouldn't be bothered. I was twice her age and then some, and there were only a select few that knew about our relationship. The last thing I needed was for word to get back to her family, and I didn't think that a casual meeting in a grocery store was covered by the same secrecy vows that applied to confession.

"Well, I've been busy—working a lot, haven't been able to make it."

It was answer enough for him or he was smarter than I expected, because he seemed placated or just tired of the scene and had seen through the ruse.

"Okay, well I expect to see you soon," he said like he was going to hold her to her word. Faith materializes in strange fashion, at times. The padre grabbed a package of hamburger, and gave me a smile as he walked away.

I smiled back, trying not to overdo it; wishing that it had been Friday and he'd been at the seafood counter instead, and the whole thing would have never happened. I breathed a sigh of relief, thinking that it had all gone rather well.

She looked at me and just grinned that silly grin that attracted me to her in the first place, and I shook my head in disbelief.

"You stand way over there."

"What are you talking about?"

"I don't want to be struck by that lightning bolt when it comes down. You haven't worked a Sunday in months—you just lied to a priest."

Her face turned the color of the red dye in the hamburger and she got that silly grin on her face again.

We bought a cake from the bakery department and later that night had a birthday party for my dog, with cake and ice cream, and paper birthday hats for us all. I'd always felt that pets should never be dressed in human clothing, because they have no say in the matter and it demeans their dignity, but the dog didn't seem to mind, probably since he was focused on the cake and ice cream. Rules were meant to be broken, and lately I was; at the very least, bending them all.

I don't know what she saw in me in the first place. It certainly wasn't money, I was working three jobs— restaurant manager by day, bartender at night, and doing landscaping on my days off, and could still barely make ends meet—butcher, baker, candlestick maker. At the big economic card table of life, I had been left behind, holding only aces and eights.

The landscaping gig was something I'd arranged with a rich, old, Japanese guy up in the valley who drank chardonnay in pint glasses and had more property and projects, than I really had time for, but it kept me into plenty of work. My latest assignment called for a morning meeting with the company rep who was replacing the pond liner in front of the guest house.

I buzzed myself in at the gate with my code and met Gil in the driveway. He was staring at the empty pond and already had a chardonnay going at 9:00 am.

"Do you want one? Come on, I'll get you one."

"Naw, it's still a little too early for me, thanks— maybe later this afternoon, when I'm finished."

The liner guy drove up and introduced himself and I was glad he'd steered the conversation away from the topic of the wine. Gil could be so persistent on having me join him sometimes that it bordered on annoyance.

We all walked around the giant pea gravel mountain that I'd removed from the bottom of the pond between the main house and the guest house. The large boulders, formerly at the water's edge, were all rolled up to the top, along the walkway.

"It looks good. I'll take out that old liner and put the new one in, and put the boulders back with my backhoe. How'd you get all that gravel out? Bobcat? I don't see any tracks."

"No, I hauled it out in five gallon buckets, up a two-by-six ramp. Gil wouldn't let me use any equipment in here."

He whistled and looked at the pea gravel mountain.

"Well, when I get done, you can bring those Mexicans back in here and put the gravel back in."

"They weren't Mexicans; I did it with two of my friends."

"How'd you get the boulders up there?"

"Oh those? We rolled them up the side with big pry bars."

He looked at me like I'd hit him between the eyes with one of the steel bars, and I left him standing there deprived of his consciousness, to start my next project.

Later that afternoon Gil and I were on the patio, sharing one of the bottles of the chardonnay that he drove back by the pickup load from California twice a year. It was November, but warmer than usual, especially in the sun.

"I need you to do me one more favor before you go."

"What's that?" I asked.

"Put those two Christmas wreaths that are in the garage, up on the gates out front, on your way out. I don't want people thinking I'm Jewish."

With the holiday season coming on, I had a reoccurring altruistic feeling in my head, which was about as original as they come for me. Maybe it was guilt, maybe a desire for a karma change, but the fact that I couldn't assign any particular reason to it only made it feel more genuine, and I took a certain bit of pride that I'd actually entertained the thought about doing anything without an ulterior motive— for once in my life. Anyway, I finally settled on helping out at the local soup kitchen, helping to feed the underprivileged, poor, and homeless. I figured it was as good a place as any for a start. I picked up the phone and made an appointment to work the next lunch shift they had available, which; luckily, happened to fall on my next day off. I wondered if perhaps the karma thing was already starting to pay dividends, although it still seemed a little early in the game, to go jumping to conclusions.

Monday came and I arrived at the soup kitchen, right on time. I entered through the front and saw a small lady with a clipboard standing in the hallway that led to the kitchen. Right away, I knew she was in charge— she had that look, the kind I'd seen from red-tailed hawks watching a pasture, waiting for a mouse to make a wrong move.

I walked over and introduced myself and she peered at me across the top of her glasses with an air of superiority that I didn't like from the get-go, then scanned the paper on the clipboard for my name, as if to suggest I'd somehow be lying about my reason for being there. Satisfied I'd met her perfunctory criteria of admission, she checked off my name and pointed down the hallway and added, "The kitchen is that way." No thank you, no wonderful of you to volunteer, nothing— nada, just a bony finger pointing the way to the kitchen and a dismissive, "The kitchen is that way." I hadn't expected the Nobel Prize for my efforts, but I didn't expect to be treated like some serf by the overlord of the soup kitchen, either.

I blew her whole attitude thing off temporarily and made my way back to the kitchen, arriving to the curious looks from two of the regulars from the bar where I worked part-time— a real-estate developer and a retired gynecologist, who were busy chopping veggies for a big pan of salad. They stared at me like deer caught in the headlights. The OB/GYN spoke first.

"What did you do, to end up here?"

"Nothing, I just volunteered to help out."

Again, the blank look from both.

"I didn't know you guys volunteered here."

"We didn't, it's community service for our DUIs."

"Oh yeah, I remember that," recalling how they'd both been caught downtown, only a few weeks apart, back in the summer. I was just about to make some comment, absolving myself from any responsibility for their present situation, because they hadn't been at my bar on either occasion, when the lady with the clipboard came in and told me to grab an apron and start cooking the pasta or we were going to be behind for lunch. She spun on her heels and clicked out of the room, leaving both of my friends staring at me again.

"You better get busy before the Field Marshal comes back," the developer said, and I could feel all the warm, fuzziness of my benevolence float right out the window.

As the lunch crowd started wandering in and we were setting up the buffet, she was back— barking out commands like some jackboot prison guard, adding to my angst— and I was feeling more and more like this whole damn thing had all been a bad idea, and I now just wanted to get it over with and get out of there. I looked for the silver lining in the faces in the dining room, hoping to see confirmation in the form of grateful smiles from the downtrodden mass I had come to serve, only to spot a handful of regular customers from the restaurant I managed, that I knew to be: neither homeless, nor downtrodden, by any stretch of the imagination. The audacity of these people, working the system for a free lunch when they were far from needy let the last of the air out of my big philanthropic balloon and I'd had it, but it certainly explained why my lunch sales were in a slump back at the restaurant.

I got through it and clean- up time finally arrived, along with another visit from the commandant, who pointed the bony finger again and issued her latest dictum, aimed directly at me.

"You,—clean the restrooms. The supplies are under the sink."

The retired gyno and the developer both lowered their heads and moved a little farther down the table from me. We were all still friends, but it was obvious they didn't want to sail on the same ship I was on.

I scrubbed the toilets and urinals with an angry vigor I'm sure they had never witnessed before, while I muttered obscenities; a litany that went deep into my vocabulary of such, which were reserved for only the most special occasions. I tossed the toilet bowl brush and the industrial strength 409, and the box of powdered latex gloves back under the sink without the same orderly care they had originated from. I undid my apron at the laundry bag on its metal frame there in the corner, pausing for a moment to look at the strings and wondering if they were strong enough to fashion into a garrote. Most everyone else had left by now; maybe I could sneak back into the kitchen and put a hit on the commandant, leave her to sleep with the fishes like Luca Brasi in the Godfather. I let it pass, marveling at how quickly I had transformed from a philanthropist to an attempted cold-blooded murderer, and tossed the apron into the bag with all the disdain I could muster, vowing never to darken the door of the place again.

Spring came; but the wind was still sharp and raw as it blew down off the snow on the mountains. It still felt like winter on most days with the budless dry branches of the trees in the yard, rasping together in the breeze, like the shedded skins of snakes. A blade of grass appeared here and there, giving hope, but lacking of promise. That's when she told me she was moving to the city to further her career.

If I had been a much younger man, I would have opted to go along. As it was, my chasing and following days were over. I'd have to let her go.

Two weeks later, she was backing out of the drive and raised her fingers from the wheel in an effort to wave. The gravel and dry pine needles made a crunching noise under the wheels in the half-melted ground of early April, and it left a hollow ringing in my head, the way I'd always imagined loneliness to sound. I reached down and stroked the dog's head as he stood there beside me. I could feel everything being drawn inward, collapsing on its own weight toward my center of mass like the gravitational pull from a supernova. A crow landed on a fencepost and eyed me with mutual introspection, and I nodded in his direction. The karma deal had been a complete bust. We were both witnessing the beginning or the end of something.

No Flowers for the Dead

Jay Walden

9 NO FLOWERS FOR THE DEAD

A Jack Daniels mini bottle fell from Ray Brown's coat pocket and bounced twice across the white tile floor, landing label up, facing his parole officer; bounced twice, like a proton in a supercollider; albeit, more freely and less encumbered, denying the laws of physics without any constrictions. There wasn't much discussion following the event; the guard standing just outside the door walked in and put the cuffs on him right where he sat; and off he went to county, to serve the remaining six months of his suspended sentence.

As if the six-month sentence wasn't enough of a hardship; on the day that he was released, the lady he'd hitched a ride with backed over his foot, out in the driveway of his dilapidated single wide, breaking two of his toes. Ray didn't even bother with a doctor visit for the foot— just wrapped it with an old ace bandage he'd found under the sink in his bathroom and double-bagged it with two Safeway plastic shopping bags to keep it dry; duct taping it at the top to his pant leg, to keep out the snow and the slush.

There was an uneasiness about town during that time, as shorter days gave way to longer nights and a waxing moon cast eerie shadows across the hoodoos just below the mesa. No one was sleeping well and everyone seemed to be on edge, while old ghosts roamed the streets and coyotes howled out in the abandoned, empty RV lots. The entire place had that look about it like somewhere dreams had come to die, everything contrasting in stark blacks and whites like an old Bergman movie. It was winter; it was cold as hell.

In the dull light of the afternoon, beneath gun barrel gray skies, I'd watch him hobble on a crutch up to the Sportsman to get his daily twelve pack of Budweiser; the neon green tennis ball on the tip of the crutch, seemingly the only thing of color against the dirty snow along the highway from the oil patch traffic. It was a painful thing to watch, I admit; the hobbling— the pausing every twenty yards or so— the lifting of that shopping bag covered foot, as he stopped to catch his breath. Painful, yet mesmerizing in a certain way; something that you just couldn't turn away from— like some visceral scene of a twisted car wreck or a badly broken heart. You had to hand the man one thing, he was determined to get his beer

even if there was no longer any joy left in it, even
when he had lost all hope and his life had become just
a head-on collision with mere existence.

We'd stopped selling to him a while back, just after
he'd come back from jail, figuring that he was too
much of a liability; but that's where I watched him
from— from the window there in the store where I
worked the afternoon shift— that guy that had a beer
trail in the snow, that guy that trouble followed
around like a lost puppy. Seems like a life of hard
edges were the only kind of lives some people ever
knew, and Ray was one of those people. Nobody
much likes a drunk; and even other drunks don't like
mean drunks, and Ray was one of those, too. He'd
made his share of enemies around this little town and
had the scars to prove it. Everyone had a story of
some type of "run in" with him at one time or
another and I was no exception; but I endured him
on his better days, even allowing him to occasionally
use the phone to call in to his P.O. He was something
you were going to have to contend with if you wanted
to live here— pain in the ass or not.

I can't remember a harder winter than that one. We
were locked into some cyclical, icy vortex that pushed
the temperatures to below zero for weeks on end and
showed no signs of ever breaking. The weather had
us all in a stranglehold; we were prisoners taking
refuge in what comfort warmth and shelter could

offer—all of us but Ray, who seemed to thrive on the depthlessness of decadence and despair his life was spiraling into. He carried that dark star with him wherever he went; wearing it like a badge of courage, pulling everyone and everything he came into contact with, right down into it. It hung thick in the air, like smoke from a trash fire, some evil obeah, a powerful portend of some negative augury that couldn't be ignored. It was only a matter of time before something bad was going to happen; somehow, we all just knew it.

The weather and the stingy sunlight were doing a number on me; the walls were closing in at home and I had to get out. The dog was getting restless too, and I decided to take him along and let him run, while I walked one of the oil field roads. I bundled up against the cold that morning with all the clothing I could find, the fresh skiff of snow in the driveway— so dry and powdery, that it squeaked beneath my boots like a pair of new tennis shoes on a gym floor. The truck battery struggled against the bitter, frigid air, then reluctantly ground the engine to a start.

The first thing I saw were the crows— then I saw the leg; I saw the leg sticking up out of the bar ditch. I pulled the truck to the side of the highway and turned on the flashers, and stepped outside, sending the crows tilting away on an icy wind. The dog made some type of low, guttural noise that I had never heard before, as I closed the door leaving him in the cab. I walked to the edge of the road and looked over the bank and down into the ditch. The crows lifted on the breeze that was coming at my back, circling above, like black demons carrying away a spirit they had come to claim. I knew right away it was Ray, although I couldn't see his face that was covered from snow, plastered there by the wind. I saw that ratty old jean jacket with the faux sheepskin lining and a bony, frail, blue hand protruding out the sleeve, still grasping the cardboard handle of a Budweiser 12 pack, like a talon of a hawk, and I knew it was him. His other leg was twisted beneath him, but I could see that shopping bag with the big red S, still on his foot; the bright red S like the one I used to admire on George Reeve's chest when I was a kid, the one that stood for strength and self-dignity, but this one had taken on a different meaning, more of a scarlet letter for pity and sadness. I turned my head from the sight of it, feeling like someone had sucker punched me in the gut. The arm on the gas well across the road, rose and fell with the syncopation of a beating heart, wrecking the silence, echoing like a jackhammer in my head. I got back in the truck and made a U-turn and headed home to call the sheriff. It was about all I could do.

That afternoon I need a drink. It had been a tough day; and the hour I had spent with the sheriff's deputy, giving him my statement, had taken its toll on my brain. I drove up to the Sportsman; and Adam, the owner, was the only guy in the place. I ordered a whiskey with a beer back; I was going for effect and I wanted the shortest route there. It was dim and quiet; the inside lights trying their best to compete with the dullness that poured in, from outside the windows.

As he sat my drinks on the bar, Adam gave me a you-sure- look- like- hell-look, and took a measured breath before he spoke, like he was considering whether he should speak at all.

"I heard you found Ray this morning, down in the bar ditch."

"Yeah, it was a damn sight. Looked like he had frozen to death."

"Son of a…"

I cut him off, "That's what I said."

The phone rang down at the other end of the bar and he left to answer it, leaving me to my drinks. He was far enough away that I couldn't hear the conversation. I was glad; I didn't want to talk to anyone— not, just now. I sipped the whiskey and looked around. This place used to really be something— lively, alive. Now it was just a building; a shell of its former self that the new owners hoped to bring back to life, like some Phoenix rising out of the ashes. Now it was just one of those places that had seen its time; and as time passes, it's never repeated again.

Deals were made here; friendships were forged; marriages arranged— although none that I knew that had ever lasted. They were all gone now like the dollar bills with names and places written in magic marker, that used to paper the walls; they were all gone now— memories; the lot of them, gone like all the other shit in life you can never replace. All that was left was a juke box that still took quarters, but seemed to play only sad songs.

Adam came back and tried to strike up the conversation again. I wasn't in the mood.

"You know your grandfather…"

"Sorry, I gotta go," I cut him off again and slid the beer mug and a twenty towards him.

"Well, see ya later," he said, as I headed towards the door.

"Yeah, I'll see ya." I didn't even bother to look back.

A week went by and I heard the dog bark, long before the knock on the door. I placed my hand on the dog's head and he sat; eyes laser focused on the front door, as I opened it.

I stared out through the heavy bars of the outer door at the two people on my porch.

"Mr. Walden?"

"Yes."

"I'm sergeant Garcia and this is officer Diaz, we're with the New Mexico State Police."

Well, that was an overstatement of the obvious. I certainly knew that they weren't Jehovah's Witnesses, unless that group had changed their MO to include Kevlar vests and Glocks, and I knew from the look on their faces they weren't here to ask me "If I had heard the good news."

"We'd like to ask you some questions about this past December 14th. The day you found Mr. Brown."

"Well, I've already given a statement to the sheriff's department. I really don't have anything to add."

I looked down at the dog; who was still on point, then back to the porch, to the both of them. Garcia was short, but stocky, about my height and build. He looked all business. Diaz shifted her weight, to her other foot. She was short and petite, but muscular, like a gymnast, with straight, jet black hair that stopped just above her shoulders; pretty, with big, soft brown eyes that looked disarming, like a doe. Her slacks fit like a glove. The gun on her hip and the badge on her belt added further intrigue. I knew her type; knew there were lightning bolts behind those big brown eyes; knew that she could lead a man down the primrose path, then let the air out of him, faster than a blink of an eye, if push ever came to shove; probably smile, while she was doing it. I wasn't letting them in, cold or not.

Garcia spoke again, "How did you come to find Mr. Brown that day?"

"Well, the crows. I….I saw the crows first, then the leg sticking up out of the ditch. Listen, I've already told the sheriff's department everything. Haven't you read my statement?"

"Yes, yes we have. But I'd like to just clarify a few things."

"I don't know what I could add that would help you with that."

"Well, where were you headed that particular morning?"

"I was taking the dog for a walk, I was going out walking."

I looked back down to the dog, as if he was going to nod and substantiate my story.

"One more question, then. When did you last see your grandfather?"

"I dunno, about a couple of weeks ago, I guess. I went up to his house to help him with his pellet stove, the feeder wasn't working; I changed out the motor for him."

"Are you aware of an altercation that recently took place at the Sportsman between your grandfather and Mr. Brown, while your grandfather was buying cigarettes up there?"

"No, I haven't heard anything about that."

I stood there with my best stone face, trying not to betray my emotions, wondering what Adam had started to tell me that day, before I had cut him off. None of it made any sense— grandpa had his share of vices, but smoking wasn't one of them.

"Okay. I'm going to leave you my card. Call me if you think of anything that would help. My cell number is on the back. Thank you for your time."

Garcia stepped off the porch and headed towards their unmarked car, just beyond the gate. Diaz lingered there for a second longer and looked inside, looking past me like there might be some vital clue she'd overlooked there in the hallway.

"That's a beautiful dog you have there," she said, as she smiled and looked straight at me with those doe eyes again.

"Yeah, he's a good boy; doesn't miss much, good for protection."

"Well, you two have yourselves a nice, rest of the day."

"We'll do that," I said as I put my hand on the door and watched her turn and go down the steps, those slacks moving away like every fiber in them had taken on a life of their own. I closed the door, hoping that my face wasn't red.

A week later, I was headed to town for groceries. The dog was up in the cab again; it was still bitter cold.

Down where county road 4599 met highway 173, there was a green and white Crown Vic from the San Juan County Sheriff's Department, parked to the side. As I rolled up to the intersection, the plumes from our exhausts; vaporizing in the cold, mingled, but I could see plainly into the car. The deputy was on his cell phone, and there in the back, sat grandpa. His old white Stetson was tilted down and he was looking at the floor like he was inspecting his boots. Across the seat sat a younger lady, staring out the back passenger side window toward the pasture beside the road. She looked lonely— like she was waiting for someone to appear among all those sheep out there and take her away from a place she never thought she'd be. I didn't recognize her. One thing was certain; she sure as hell didn't look anything like grandma.

Epilogue or Eulogy

10 EPILOGUE OR EULOGY

I watched a movie the other night that I had been thinking about watching for a long time, called *The Diving Bell and the Butterfly*. I watched it mainly because I was intrigued by the title.

Well, it took me a couple nights to get through it; not because it was slow, or uninteresting, or anything like that; but just because, by the time I got home and started watching it, it was already late. Nighttime is the only time you should really watch movies, unless you are a total loser and watch them during the day; but, you start watching them late at night and you're older and all, and you just fall asleep.

Anyway, the movie was based on a true story about a guy that had a stroke and couldn't talk, so he writes a book by dictating the words through blinking his eyes to the correct letters while someone recites the alphabet to him. I found myself wishing that I could write a book by blinking my eyes. Not that I would ever want to have a stroke or communicate every letter of every word by an acknowledging blink, but more like *I Dream of Jeanie*, where I blink one time and the book is done, and it's good, real good, a best seller. Instead, I struggle with it. I struggle for the right word or words; I struggle whether a comma should go here, a period there. I struggle with it like a prospector hacking at the smallest vein of silver with blunt instruments of steel, hoping; always, that it will lead to something bigger; or perhaps better—gold, perhaps.

Charles Bukoski wrote (and he's a pretty great writer of poetry) that if you have to sit there and rewrite it again and again, then don't do it. Unless it comes unmasked out of your heart and mouth, don't do it.

Sometimes it does; sometimes it comes out unmasked, but sometimes it doesn't and I sit painfully rereading, rewriting, and editing something that I thought was just absolutely wonderful the day before. Maybe I'm not ready; maybe, one day when it is time and I have been chosen, it will do it by itself. Until then, this will have to be the way I get it done; hopefully, it's good enough. We'll see, we'll see.

ABOUT THE AUTHOR

Jay Walden is an avid fly fisherman, hunter, and Ray Wylie Hubbard fan. He lives in Navajo Dam, New Mexico.

Made in the USA
Middletown, DE
28 March 2023